W9-AAR-780

A Must-Have Reference Guide to Your Astrological Self

The key to understanding your horoscope is understanding your birth chart's house placements. That's why you need a detailed, easy-to-use guide like *The House Book*.

If you know what houses your planets call "home"—but you aren't sure where to look for answers about what it all means—*The House Book* casts a clear light on what can be a confusing subject.

If you are a practicing astrologer, *The House Book* offers a fresh new look at planetary placements—one that relies on intensive research into real charts rather than preconceived assumptions from other books.

With chart comparisons and examples culled from hundreds of charts, *The House Book* focuses entirely on the key information revealed by the house placements in your horoscope. Use it as your definitive guide to your astrological self, as revealed by the houses.

About the Author

An intense spiritual awakening at the age of nineteen led Stephanie Camilleri to study Buddhism, Hinduism, the Bible, yoga, astrology, past lives, Gurdjieff, Scientology, quantum physics, the Tarot, and other paths to an understanding of the meaning of existence.

Her study of astrology began in the 1960s before the advent of the New Age movement, when information on the subject was mostly limited to classic tomes in dusty bookstores. After four years of intense investigation convinced her of astrology's validity, she began years of effort to discover how and why.

Unable to find a book that resolved the many questions and contradictions regarding the astrological houses, she decided to research and write one herself. The result of that ten-year quest is *The House Book*.

To Write to the Author

If you wish to contact the author, please write to her in care of Llewellyn Worldwide, and we will forward your request. Both the author and the publisher appreciate hearing from you and learning of your enjoyment of this book and how it has helped you. Llewellyn Worldwide cannot guarantee that every letter written to the author can be answered, but all will be forwarded. Please write to:

Stephanie Camilleri
c/o Llewellyn Worldwide
P.O. Box 64383, Dept. K108–2
St. Paul, MN 55164-0383, U.S.A.

Please enclose a self-addressed, stamped envelope or $1.00 to cover costs. If outside the U.S.A., enclose international postal reply coupon.

The House Book

Stephanie Camilleri

The Influence
of the Planets
in the Houses

1999
Llewellyn Publications
St. Paul, MN 55164-0383 U.S.A.

FIRST EDITION
First Printing, 1999

Cover design: Anne Marie Garrison
Editing and page layout: Marguerite Krause

Library of Congress Cataloging–in–Publication Data

Camilleri, Stephanie.   1938–
   The house book / Stephanie Camilleri.   — 1st ed.
     p.   cm.
   ISBN 1–56718–108–2
   1. Houses (Astrology)   I. Title.
  BF1716.C35 1999   99–20578
                                                    CIP

Llewellyn Worldwide does not participate in, endorse, or have any authority or responsibility concerning private business transactions between our authors and the public.
   All mail addressed to the author is forwarded but the publisher cannot, unless specifically instructed by the author, give out an address or phone number.

Llewellyn Publications
A Division of Llewellyn Worldwide, Ltd.
P.O. Box 64383, Dept. K108–2
St. Paul, MN 55164-0383, U.S.A.

Contents

Preface:
About This Book

Some years ago, I became curious to find out more about the eighth house. The material on the subject in my books was ambiguous, and no matter what I read, I couldn't get any real sense of it. It seemed to me that the authors who wrote about this house did not deal with it thoroughly. There it was, tucked away in a remote corner of the right side of the chart, assigned to an odd assortment of prerogatives: death, taxes, other people's money, occult experiences, dreams. Now and then there was a hint that it might have something to do with sex.

Thinking that I would have a look at it myself by means of some charts of famous people, I thumbed through my collection of famous charts (not large at that time), and found that Marilyn Monroe, Jean Harlow, Humphrey Bogart, and Gary Cooper all had planets on the cusp of the eighth house. Well!

Those were famous people; perhaps the story would be different if I scanned the eighth houses of common, garden-variety charts; those of clients, friends, and family. I found that, with these charts as well, planets in the eighth house—particularly on the cusp, or in the seventh near the eighth-house cusp—invariably demonstrated charisma—the more planets, the more intense the charisma. There was a compelling quality about these people that went beyond their looks, and beyond the nature or importance of their work or position. It didn't matter which planets they were, although I suspected that the charisma took its particular tone from the specific planets.

Among those with planets in the eighth house (or the seventh house near the cusp of the eighth house) were John Barrymore, Rudolph Valentino, Charlie Chaplin, Marlene Dietrich, Henry Fonda, Greta Garbo, Errol Flynn, Carole Lombard, William Holden, Ava Gardner, Brigitte Bardot, Rudolf Nuryev, Bob Dylan, John Lennon, both Baba Ram Dass, *and* Timothy Leary. Among writers, I found Arthur Rimbaud, Charles Baudelaire, Georges Sand, Charlotte Brontë, Walt Whitman, Percy Shelley, George (Lord) Byron, Miguel de Cervantes, Voltaire, and Dante Alighieri. Among artists were Michelangelo, Rembrandt, Edgar Degas, Auguste Rodin, Henri de Toulouse-Lautrec, and Marc Chagall.

Significant historical figures include Patrick Henry, Napoleon, Joan of Arc, Robert E. Lee, Dwight D. Eisenhower, General George Rommel, Juan Peron, Joseph

Smith (the Mormon leader), Mussolini, Hitler, Mao Tse Tung, Ronald Reagan, John F. Kennedy (as well as his First Lady Jacqueline), and Billy the Kid. Of course, The Kid's chart has to be taken with a grain of salt because it is based on sketchy data, but given the evidence for charisma evoked by planets in the eighth, the strange passion and intense loyalty that this innocuous-looking but deadly teenager evoked in his neighbors on the frontier would seem to testify to the accuracy of this chart.

Well, I thought, if the traditional view of the eighth house is so lacking, perhaps the traditional view of the other houses is not as substantial as one would wish, either. I was tired of trying to find a book that explained the nature of the planets in the houses to my satisfaction. At that point, I decided to do the research and write it myself.

I started with the charts of roughly six hundred well-known individuals (a number that increased to twelve hundred before I was done), plus those of two to three hundred persons whom I knew personally. I chose the charts of the famous according to how much I knew about their personal lives as well as their public lives, and how accurate the chart was thought to be. Sometimes I included charts that were not so reliable if they were of women or people of color, individuals unfortunately still in the vast minority in "famous" chart collections although this imbalance has been somewhat adjusted in recent years. I indicated the not-so-reliable charts with an asterisk throughout my notes, to remind me that the data was shaky; a double asterisk if it was really questionable (Lois Rodden's "dirty data"). In this way, I was able to combine knowledge gleaned from a lifetime of reading biographies and history with my knowledge of astrology. I was assisted greatly during the course of my research by collections of charts that came out at that time; those of Lois Rodden, Stephen Erlewine, Mark Penfield, and the Gauquelins, to all of whom I am very grateful.

A Cautionary Note

Sensitive topics in this kind of work include sexual preference, likelihood of divorce, mental instability, criminal tendencies, and the possibility of early or violent death. I have not withheld any information, but cannot emphasize strongly enough that one or two indications of a trait *do not by any means* provide a certainty. There must be *many such indications* for any one trait to be taken as a given. Phrases like "tend to," "inclined to," or "partial tendency to" are meant as pointers for astrologers to keep an eye on that trait, looking for other indicators that strengthen or mitigate it. Newcomers to astrology, *be careful with this!* Like anything with power, astrology has the potential to hurt as well as help. Our job is to help our clients, friends, and families find a way to live and grow. We don't have to tell them everything we see— or think we see.

In recent years, astrologers have been trying to get away from the terms "bad" and "good" for aspects, positions, and locations of planets in signs or houses. In general, this is a good idea, because we are all trying to get past the limiting and often erroneous generalizations that have been handed down to us from the past. However, the opposite approach, which calls for a plentiful use of psychological or spiritual terminology, a disinclination to be either negative or specific, and an accent on healing, is not all that useful in *delineating* charts, and is not what you will find here. This book is written from an external perspective of perceived personality, not from an internal perspective of psychological mechanisms. Those mechanisms may be the cause of the perceived personality, and we may desire to heal and be healed, but apart from a few suggestions to parents, this book is about traits, not prescriptions for changing them.

The aim here is to be particular, with the understanding that other factors must constantly be taken into consideration. The color aqua may look green next to orange, but blue beside a Kelly green. Beauty is in the eye of the beholder, and the interpretation of a chart is in the mind and heart of the astrologer, not the writer of the reference book. My job is to give you the greenest green, the bluest blue, the reddest red, the blackest black, the whitest white. Your job is to use this palette to paint realistic portraits of your clients. It wouldn't do you much good if I give you a pastel green, or gray in place of black. It is for you to mix the colors for each individual chart, as you see fit.

He, She, and They

Please forgive the awkward grammar that arises from the use of the third person plural in place of the singular. Referring to everyone and anyone as "he" just isn't fair to half the world's population. To try to even things up by using "he" half the time and "she" the other half is, for me, a tiresome distraction. In *Heaven Knows What*, Grant Lewi used the second person "you," which avoided the Scylla of gender but plunged into the Charybdis of context; that is, it works fine when doing one's own chart, but when doing someone else's chart, the constant use of "you" is irritating. If someone can come up with a better way around our terrible English gender gap, they would certainly be rendering us all a great service.

Author's Data

For those interested in the chart behind the voice, the author was born May 24, 1938, at 1:28 A.M. Central Standard Time in Willmar, Minnesota; latitude 45N07, longitude 95W03 (while the great and enduring Uranus-Neptune trine was still in Earth signs).

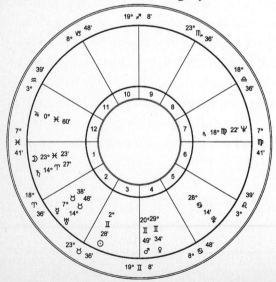

How to Use
This Book

The best and the worst effects of the planets in the houses have been outlined here. The actual operation in most charts will be somewhere in between. For those who are reading to better understand their friends and loved ones, the more extreme manifestations of both difficult and easy aspects must be taken with caution. Most people are neither monster nor genius, which they would appear to be if the aspect is taken at full force—a condition that requires a number of supporting positions and aspects.

This is even more important to keep in mind when reading for purposes of self-discovery, as we humans have a hard time seeing ourselves clearly. Some tend to see only the best about themselves (Taurus and Leo) while others tend to concentrate on the worst (Pisces and Virgo). These are the extremes of the elements you contain within you. You will probably never touch either the heights or the depths you contain, but it is good to know what they are. To know the worst truth is to be given the power to challenge and overcome it. To know the best is to be given a goal towards which to strive.

It is my personal belief that the soul comes into the world for specific purposes, much as a student enrolls at a university in order to get a degree. In my view, the circumstances of birth are chosen by the soul, just as a series of courses is chosen by a student, based on how far and how fast they wish to advance and the amount and nature of preparation they bring to their studies. The more difficult the life situation, the more challenging the course and the greater the opportunity for growth and experience.

Where the planets are not present to give those things that are desired, one must replace them with determination and will power, planning and cunning. If you are a woman with Mars in the second, bent on having a successful career, and you read that very few women with Mars in the second have ever made it to glory, just tell yourself, "Here's the one who will!" At least you'll know what you're up against.

Astrology is no more than a series of markers or milestones, nothing more than a set of dials on the dashboard of your little boat, working its way to the further shore across the great sea of life. It can show the kind of tools a person has to work with, and the nature of the challenges they will face, but it can say nothing about the amount of will power or guts that an individual will bring with them. Nothing in astrology is written in stone. The human will and spirit has ever been and will ever be the final word.

The Moon Through the Houses

The Moon is the only planet in astrology that belongs to the earth alone. In fact, it is part of the mechanism of the earth. More than any other external factor, it is responsible for the existence and cycles of organic life on earth—cycles of birth, growth, and death, the propagation of life forms and the procreation of species. All the planets contribute their individual energies to this process, but the Moon creates the greenhouse of the sublunar realm where these energies can be collected and maintained at the necessary levels of vibration for organic life to reseed and maintain itself.

Since the Moon is the closest planet to the earth, it is the fastest-moving from our perspective, spending about two-and-a-half days in each sign and circling the zodiac in just under twenty-eight days.

The Moon rules the birth and the period of life up to about four years of age, when humans are helpless and completely under the control and protection of their parents. This is the impressionable period before conscious memory takes hold, and when the basic emotional nature is set.

The Moon also has much to do with the immune system and with periodic cycles of health that lead to minor illnesses such as colds, bouts of flu, and some allergies, illnesses that are basically natural cleansing processes. It influences the periodic cycles of fertility in women, is involved in the strength or weakness of a woman's sexual apparatus and function, and says much in a woman's chart about her health in general. In the body, it rules most of the glands, particularly the lymph and thyroid, as well as the white corpuscles in the blood.

Traditionally, the Moon in a chart speaks of the emotional nature. It rules relationships with women, and with the mother in particular. It is very strong in the water signs, especially in Cancer, which it is said to rule. It is not very strong in air signs, tending to rationalize feelings to too great an extent, and in fire signs it has a hard time providing the sympathetic connection to the hearts and needs of others that is one of the Moon's primary functions. Among the earth signs, it is very good in Taurus, not so good in Virgo, and it is at its weakest of all positions in Capricorn.

The Moon in the First House

With a rising Moon there is a powerful hunger for personal significance and strong intuition about the trend of future events. Once the restlessness and moodiness of this position is brought under control, this can lead to amazing achievements.

People with this position are generally too sensitive for their own good, and tend to go to extremes, especially in youth. They usually have large, expressive eyes, a wide, expressive mouth, and a responsive face. They have a hard time masking thoughts and feelings, which flit rapidly across the face (though less so in Scorpio or Capricorn). They are inclined to think out loud, to speak whatever is passing through their minds at the moment, no matter how out of context or inappropriate it may seem to their listeners. Actually, they are always talking to themselves.

People with a rising Moon tend to marry young and may fall in love too easily throughout their lives. Each new love does not diminish the emotional hold of past loves, though, which can make their love life pretty complicated until they begin to understand themselves. They love best those companions who cherish them for what they are, allow them to ramble on, and then set limits for them. They know that limits must be set, but have a hard time setting them for themselves.

They are pretty much incapable of objectivity. Even sympathy is hard for them as they do not see others clearly although they can *become* them, or feel them, that is, identify with them through empathy. This can make them appear cold when they turn away from persons or situations that are painful, because they have no buffers to protect them from the intensity of their own responses. They are generally not thinkers, because their intuition is capable of giving them all they require to grasp concepts and figure things out. They can come up with answers without any notion of how they arrived at them.

Extremely self-conscious in youth, they feel that everyone is looking at them and thinking about them all the time. They have a hard time getting over this, always giving themselves more importance in the scheme of things than is realistic. Yet this quality invests them with a natural authority, so that people tend to look to them for answers, particularly during a crisis. They are so self-oriented because their minds constantly fill with ideas and images and they must continually seek outlets or they become mentally and emotionally clogged.

They may seem unrealistic to less sensitive and less imaginative people. In fact, given a few other aspects in that direction, they may acquire a reputation as a first-class eccentric. However, they generally have a circle of friends who enjoy their idiosyncrasies, for although they appear to be paying no attention to anyone but themselves, their listening powers are tremendous. They can absorb more about others than most, and are capable of astonishing feats of memory and thoughtfulness. Even so, they are hard on intimates as they require constant outlets for their ideas and emotions, and so require a large social circle so they can go from one to another as they wear out each person.

They are usually very expressive in art, writing, speaking, acting, and music, but frequently have a hard time staying with one effort long enough to bring anything to fruition. They need a strong Saturn in their chart or they will blow all over the pond. They are usually very clever at spotting trends and coming up with the "next big thing" that will please the public. However, they will usually need disciplined partners to help them take advantage of this gift or nothing will come of it.

If harsh aspects from Mercury show mental or emotional problems, there may be a danger of mental illness with this position, in which other people appear only as mirrors that reflect back the self. Surrounded by self images, they can find no objective reality to grasp hold of. At some point indicated by progressions, mental or emotional illness may even claim them as a permanent casualty.

In general, though, the rising Moon gives a great potential for growth and change throughout the lifetime. After the roller coaster ride of youth slows down a bit, these people should be able to get a grip on themselves and put their great gifts to use.

The Moon in the Second House

There is a quality of reserve or silence to this position. Still waters run deep. The Moon here absorbs impressions but does not easily find ways to give them outward expression. This is a good placement for artists and writers who will use their craft to translate their impressions into effective ideas and images. Generally well-spoken in any given situation, people with this Moon will usually not be the first to speak, nor will they speak often, or long. They delight in plain, straightforward speech, direct and to the point. Sometimes they are masters of the witty aside. Garrulousness with this position is an indication of serious sexual frustration.

Sexual fulfillment is extremely important to this position. They are generally powerfully attracted to potential sexual partners. If, for some reason, this attraction does not bring them a fulfilling relationship, it will cause a variety of mental and emotional problems. Women with this Moon often have large breasts; both sexes seem to radiate sexual energy. They are very aware of sexuality in others from an early age. The Moon's sign and the aspects to it from other planets will show whether this is a positive and healthy development, or if it leads to repression and a fear or hatred of sex on the one hand, or to a cynical exploitation of it on the other. In our sexually confused society, children with this location need a lot of healthy physical love in babyhood to avoid the pitfalls that a second house Moon can bring to those without a strong early foundation.

Men with Moon in the second house will be attracted to sexual partners by their sexuality, by their possessions, or both. If the Moon is in a fixed sign, he will be too possessive of partners. Some men deal with the sexual pressures of this position by turning to prostitutes.

Some women with this position are so afraid of sex that they hide behind ugly clothes, unbecoming hair styles, and off-putting facial expressions. Others revel in it and have no qualms about taking anyone who pleases them to bed, maintaining all the while a cool, virginal facade and a total and lifelong silence on the subject, even to best friends (whose partners may number among their conquests). Then there are others who advertise their sexuality through tempting clothing and attitudes, whose only real pleasure is the material gain they receive from their lovers. Conversely, some may be the prey of such persons.

For men, the intense sexuality of this position can lead to homosexual episodes, though more often it leads to a fear of potential homosexual tendencies in themselves, or a paranoia towards homosexuals and a fear of possible homosexual advances from friends and acquaintances. With the Moon in Cancer, the sexuality may be so responsive and intense that it results in bisexuality or bisexual episodes.

Love is very necessary to these people, although it may or may not be directly connected with sexuality. If other aspects show it, they may make fools of themselves for love. Powerful attractions occur that are hard to deny and may last for years. Artists with this Moon position will seek a "Muse" or love object for their talent to revolve around.

A second house Moon creates a strong instinct for acquiring money and property. For less highly evolved souls, this might mean acquisition by illegal or immoral means. On a higher level, there may be an appearance of disinterested love or affection that somehow results in the fortuitous acquisition of wealth or property. The most highly-evolved souls will cheerfully acknowledge their love of beautiful, valuable things and an interest in acquiring the means to obtain them. Along with the acceptance of this acquisitiveness as a natural desire goes a willingness to use property for the benefit of others and the desire to take good care of it.

If there are stressful aspects to the Moon, there may be long bouts of poverty, particularly in childhood or youth. This can result in intensified efforts to acquire money and property later. It can also result in a painful awareness of the inherent injustice of a social structure that allows the rich to get richer while the poor get poorer, and an interest in the reform of property laws.

The Moon in the Third House

The Moon in the third house gives a hunger for self expression, and for community and an easy give and take relationship with others. Without afflictions, these people express themselves easily and early in life, choosing their words carefully with attention to the effect on their audience, and are natural and spontaneous in speaking to groups. Usually humorous and entertaining, they are not inclined to reveal themselves or their inner workings, but aim to communicate by means of stories, anecdotes, and jokes. If they are artists, their works will show this, plays and novels being a series of episodes. If teachers, they use anecdotes to get a point across.

They are usually pleasant companions, rarely putting pressure on others. They are very sympathetic and understanding of the human condition. Throughout their lives, they accumulate stories of people and keep account of the sum total of valor and suffering. They are quite objective about their own place in the scheme of things, and are usually modest and self-deprecating. If the Sun is in Cancer or Virgo, or either of these two signs is rising, there may be too much modesty. They will not think well enough of themselves, or will be afraid to push forward in life, continually asking that others evaluate them.

With the Moon in Capricorn, lack of understanding can damage the rapport with others. There will be the desire to entertain, but not the understanding of how to do it. Stories will be off the mark. With bad Saturn or Pluto aspects, bitterness, self pity, and jealousy may distort their evaluation of their relation to the world. Their anecdotes will reflect this, the point of every story being how he or she "showed them." There may be times when their balance and good humor prevail and other times when the humor is sour and self pitying. If other factors in their charts show a drinking problem or mental/emotional troubles, this lunar placement will intensify it.

With the Moon in Scorpio, emotions may get in the way at times, leaving them silent in groups, wishing they could join in spontaneously but finding it difficult to begin.

Those with the Moon in the third house are very people-oriented. They believe in the old adage that "the proper study of Man is Mankind." They often become teachers, or teach part time for the fun of it, because they communicate so easily.

Men with this Moon placement will be attracted to witty, communicative partners: teachers, writers, librarians, or students. With the Moon in Aquarius, Gemini,

Pisces, or Sagittarius, they may find their partners hard to hold. Women with the Moon in these signs will find it hard to stay faithful, at least in youth. It generally indicates a talkative and/or intelligent mother.

The Moon in the Fourth House

The Moon in the fourth house gives a great hunger for emotional security. People with this position will pour all their emotional energies into securing the steady, protective maternal kind of love that they must have in order to go out and achieve something. Love relationships are dangerous for them because they do not play around and can be wounded to the depths of their being by the apparent treachery of loved ones whose emotional needs are not as deep as their own. This attitude can be repressive to others. They are the children who required an official "best friend." If they feel secure in the love at home, they can rise to great heights of accomplishment as they have a deep instinct for people and business, and their need for security is a powerful driving force. If the Moon is in an earth sign, physical security is also very important to them, and they will do whatever it takes to own land and have a substantial savings account.

There is a shyness with this Moon, a fear of the limelight. In a creative chart it will show one who plans or works behind the scenes; if they actually step onto the stage, it will be only under the utmost creative compulsion. They usually feel completely at ease only in the immediate family circle and among long-time friends. They are self-conscious in front of groups, and they are always cautious about revealing their true feelings about things. This insecurity gives them an instinctive identification with underdogs and all victims of injustice. The rights of individuals are important to them. Someone victimized by a machine-like social institution can cause them to stick their necks out where nothing else will.

They go through emotional cycles and have dark moods during which they brood over the betrayal of lovers, the ingratitude of family or friends, and man's inhumanity to man (or woman). In some cases, their standards of devotion are so high that they turn aside from all long-term emotional commitments out of fear of being hurt. Also, if betrayed, their love can turn to hate, and they will bear grudges and be exceedingly vindictive towards former loved ones.

They need to be babied at times. Men with this position usually want their wives to stay at home and keep house and not go out to work or have a separate circle of friends. It may mean that the mother was more important than the father, or played the father's role in some way.

The Moon in the Fifth House

This is a very strong and positive position for the Moon, as it is often trine both the ascendant and the midheaven. It gives a strong sense of self and a competitive nature with a hunger for creative self-expression. These people have a great desire to accomplish something; to be better looking, smarter, make more money quicker, or turn out more work faster than anybody else. There is a great desire for victory against competition, yet not to the point of damaging competitors. They know instinctively that a strong competitor is the best means to their own improved performance.

Men with this position will be attracted to and try to win the prettiest girl, the one all the others want. A woman with this position wants to be that girl, and probably will be. She will want to be more than that, though, and will probably try to handle both a career and kids. These people have a great love of children. They make good teachers, particularly of small children.

They also love sports and games. They like sports where they can participate, as well as watch and take sides. They generally like to gamble, although they aren't inclined to become steady gamblers because they don't enjoy losing.

The Moon in the fifth house adds an aura of self-confidence that is very attractive to others. Romance will be very important and there will be romantic episodes from early in life (though they may be quite brief if the Moon is square its dispositor). If the Moon is trine the ascendant or a rising planet, the personality is very powerful and attractive to others. There is a theatrical flair to it that is excellent for actors, politicians, salesmen, entertainers, and athletes. It gives the power to attract an audience, or a broad circle of admirers. It is also good for novelists, screenwriters, playwrights, directors, impresarios, and others of that sort, because it gives a theatrical imagination.

Men with this placement of the Moon will be attracted to younger lovers. Both sexes have a lifelong sense of romance and will be on the lookout for romantic adventures or, rather, for adventures with romantic overtones, for the love of home and family usually prevents real philandering. They just want to be assured from time to time that they can get it if they want it. Once youth is past, they are generally too busy being creative in a thousand other ways to keep playing romantic games. In an earth or water sign, there is bound to be a "green thumb" that can grow anything. Actually there is likely to be at least one hobby at which they excel, and possibly several.

The Moon in the Sixth House

With the Moon here there is an immense hunger for significance, for worthwhile work and service. There is a great capacity for hard work, but unless other aspects show it, these people are not often self-starters. They usually need someone to work for, someone they respect. They have a strong desire for accomplishment, but by someone else's lights, at least in youth. Unless other chart factors indicate the contrary, they may lack the self-confidence to work on their own, setting their own standards. There is a great desire for an ideal boss, one who will set standards and limits, who appreciates hard work and rewards results. Unfortunately, this is an ideal that is not often found, which causes them a great deal of tension that can result in disorders of the stomach or the glands.

Often these people are not paid what they are worth. There is a selfless aspect here, a desire to work for the love of it, purely for the results and not for personal gain. Either that, or the effort of asking for raises in salary brings up issues of self-worth that they find painful to deal with. Therefore they often wind up working for non-profit organizations, volunteering in charity organizations, or even going into religious orders; sometimes because they believe in the work, and sometimes because this way they can avoid issues of self worth (and possibly both).

These people are deeply concerned with their purpose in life and will continually keep an account of their record, which creates a lot of internal tension. "Did I do as much as I could have done? Would Thomas Merton (or Albert Schweitzer, or Mother Teresa) have done more?"

Often, in childhood, they felt they could get their mother's love only by proof of accomplishment, hard work, and success. The attitude may persist, consciously or subconsciously, that love is the reward of hard work, not likely to come for free (and when it does come for free, it must not be the real thing). If the Moon is under pressure of bad aspects, this constant striving can cause a health breakdown at some point, resulting in a total inability to work, generally because of a desperate need for approval.

As they get older, these stresses can lead to one of two things. On one hand, they may finally realize that no boss will ever fulfill the ideal they have been seeking, and that if they are to function as effectively as they wish they must figure out some way to be their own boss and serve humanity in their own way, a process that may involve a good deal of emotional suffering and painful self-understanding. On the other hand, if they continue to work for someone else, they will probably stop looking for perfection sooner or later, and come finally to view their co-workers like family, forgiving them their faults and working to bring about a happy family atmosphere at work, socializing outside of work with colleagues, organizing office birthday parties, and company picnics.

If the Moon is close to the seventh house cusp, or if it is trine the ascendant, these people will be more aware of public needs and will be more likely to rise to a position of importance.

The Moon in the Seventh House

Here the Moon gives a hunger for response. The life may seem to be fated, or strongly marked by destiny. People with the Moon here, opposite the Ascendant and square the Midheaven, often seem to struggle all their lives against a tide of circumstance that forces them into the same kind of situation over and over. This is wearying, but develops emotional strength. Others do not struggle against the tide of destiny, but learn to flow with it. They may avoid much suffering in this way, but also may not develop as much emotionally and spiritually.

People with this Moon are very aware of and sensitive to public opinion. They often wish they could change themselves and be more what others seem to want them to be. Sometimes it works the other way, and they become very defensive of their individuality.

They have a strong feeling for the needs and desires of the public and, given other factors, can achieve success as a public figure or a performer. Even if they do not rise to a level where they can address the public and manipulate them, they may have a sense of public destiny, an inner call to serve the public in some way. Usually they develop a strong personal style in response to the sensation of being the focus of public attention. Where other chart factors show a public career, this position gives a big push towards success. These people feel married to the public, and often have a hard time with personal relationships as their true partner is their audience or constituency.

With the Moon in Capricorn, there may be a Peter Pan complex—a rejection of the ugliness and phoniness of adult behavior, a clinging to the purity and values of childhood. These people often become teachers or counselors of children, or work with or for them in some way. It takes them much longer to grow up than others, and they shouldn't marry young. Sometimes they never marry.

A seventh-house Moon gives a special emphasis to the relationship with the mother. In some cases, she is gone early in life (dies or deserts), so that they spend the rest of their lives seeking a substitute. Or she may acquire too much control over their lives, in some cases becoming their only true partner. Other factors will tell which variation is more likely (absence or death of the father, for example).

These people are not usually successful in attempts to choose a mate; usually they are chosen by others.

There can be many strange and fateful circumstances surrounding their mating. If they feel they are being forced to marry against their will or have doubts about the marriage, they should certainly wait until they feel more positive because it is probable that marriage won't be good for them under the circumstances.

In a woman's chart, this lunar placement may be a partial testimony to homosexuality, bisexuality, or homosexual episodes, because the powerful need for feminine love and affection causes them to keep seeking it until they find it. Mothers of children with a seventh-house Moon should be aware of the difficulties that can follow a lack of physical affection in childhood, particularly the first four years. At the same time, they must be careful not to cling to this child as they grow older, but give them the freedom they need to learn through trial and error to make the right choice of their own companions.

The Moon in the Eighth House

With this placement there is a deep, silent hunger for warmth, contact, and sexual response. These people are strongly attracted to women, and for both men and women, relationships with women may be the most important in their lives. They usually relate more easily to women than to men.

This location of the Moon is a partial testimony to homosexuality or bisexuality. In a woman's chart, it may draw her to another woman as a partner. In a man's chart, it may give him the female point of view to the extent that he functions more as a woman than as a man in a relationship with another man. In any case, there is much thinking and feeling about sexuality, and there probably will be at least one peculiar sex-related experience in their lives. Children with this aspect should be watched carefully so they don't become the victim of a child molester (check for Moon or Venus contacts with Pluto or Saturn).

These people are intensely warm and feeling towards friends and family, and usually toward all humanity and other creatures as well, often seeing a need where others would not. They are capable of surprising sensitivity and deeds of generosity, spurred by these insights. However, they tend to suffer at other times because no one seems to respond to their needs in the same way, not realizing that they are different in this respect from most people. Some, men especially, may wear a mask of indifference to hide their warmth and sensitivity, as well as their sexuality. This causes deep suffering because their means of contact with the warm creature life they need and the joy of give and take with others are cut off.

People with an eighth-house Moon often experience a poignant connection between love and death. Their lives are often permanently marked by the loss, or threat of loss, of a loved one in death, and they are always aware of the drama that death creates in life. Often they are drawn to the occult in an effort to see beyond the veil that separates the living and the dead, or to find an explanation for spontaneous ESP experiences.

If other aspects in the chart corroborate, there may be much suffering caused by the mother, wife, or both, either by loss through death, sexual affairs that destroy family unity, or coldness due to a subconscious fear of the possible sexual implications of ordinary maternal intimacy. Some women with this Moon position will compensate for a lack of warmth in their own childhood with too great a display of feeling towards their own children, or "smother love." Or they may seek to fill the void left by their own mother with lesbian relationships.

This location of the Moon inclines towards what is called "second sight" or heightened psychic awareness. Dreams are important to these people; their psyche often communicates with them through dreams. They may have an uncanny ability to predict future events.

The Moon in the eighth house is a good position for writers of words or music and for actors, because these careers are ways of translating the sensuality and sympathy into widely accepted forms and, better yet, are means for rousing the same sensitivities and responses in the hearts of others.

The Moon in the Ninth House

These people love truth and adventure and can never get enough of either. To them, home is where the hat is, or the heart, and is not connected to land or buildings (unless the Moon is in an earth sign). They are never content to sit by the fire—at least, not for long.

Men with this aspect are inclined to be attracted to partners from faraway places, or from a culture very different from their own. They may also have a hard time holding onto them. Most men with this position of the

Moon lose a partner or important love relationship at least once, and possibly more than once (unless the Moon is in Cancer or Capricorn). Often, the relationship seems to fade away while he is involved elsewhere, at work, or on a long business trip. Women with this location of the Moon are adventurous and daring, even if they hide it, and will strike out for faraway places or adventure at least once or twice in their lives.

These people are usually good storytellers and appreciate good stories. They want to hear about life from the horse's mouth almost as much as they want to experience it themselves and tell others about it. They are attracted to various systems of thought, and will try one after another, seeking the truth within each as they seek the essence of life in adventures. They are somewhat inclined to lose sight of goals and get carried away by passing enthusiasms unless there are balancing aspects in the chart. Their search for the meaning of life can lead them into almost any field. They may be drawn to the ministry, but be put off by its restrictions on their freedom.

With the Moon in a water sign, they will have deep insights into natural laws. In Capricorn, they may be attracted to a public career. In air, they will be able to see into human nature. In fire, they may work to become a virtuoso of some sort.

In any sign, they will have insights into life often enough so that seeking and nourishing their insights will be part of their lives. Trips will be important to them. Many of the important events of their lives will occur on or because of a trip to a faraway place, or because of a visit from, someone from far away.

This Moon position often gives a wise, religious, or refined mother, one who stimulates their interest in knowledge, learning, and the truth; although, if there are bad aspects, the mother may also bring grief, have mental or emotional problems, or a life situation that will isolate them from her in some way. Thus enters the element of search, especially in a man's chart.

These people like to teach, but often lack the patience for it.

The Moon in the Tenth House

Here the Moon gives a hunger for success, prestige, and renown. People with the Moon at the top of the chart often have most success working with or for women. A woman—whether their mother or someone else—may influence their choice of a career and help them get started.

Women with this position rarely remain financially dependent on husbands. Usually they start early to earn their own living, and even with children, generally keep on working, often managing a full-time career. They are usually good at organizing and managing others, especially other women. Often, they marry men who depend on them, at least the first time, as it is a pleasure, at first, to be looked up to as the organizer and protector. Later, they usually want to escape from such a relationship; not to one where they are dependent on a man, but to a wider sphere for their managerial talents. They don't relish dependency, and have little respect for those who do. With the

Moon in a water sign, they may understand emotional dependency—but they will still want out.

Men with the Moon in the tenth often marry women with more drive and ambition for them than they have for themselves. Often, they will go into business as a team, with her providing the ideas and drive. In any case, she generally "wears the pants." Such men often have strong-minded and ambitious mothers as well. It is usually best for men with this lunar position to wait until their careers are established before they marry. This way, they will meet their mates working in their own career field and the working relationship will be the foundation of their emotional lives. Whatever their relationships with women, they will find it hard to keep them private. Somehow the spotlight always finds them.

People with the Moon in the tenth house have a feeling for the public. They know instinctively what "the people" need and want and are clever at molding themselves into an image that will arouse public enthusiasm. The public gives its heart to those who somehow can express what it feels but cannot express for itself.

This placement is a very strong testimonial to a public career, although supportive aspects are necessary to make it permanent and successful because there are facets other than popularity that must be present. With just a tenth house Moon there may be too great a hunger for popularity for its own sake. If so, they may appear to have no strong will of their own.

With squares, oppositions, or inconjuncts to the Moon, there is a tendency to a loss of self-control under pressure that can bring unfortunate results.

The Moon in the Eleventh House

People with this Moon placement seem to take things for granted. They appear to know what they want and proceed towards it gradually and evenly, without qualms, ignoring obstacles that would stop others. Even if they have little or nothing, they behave as though money were no object. They may be born into comfortable circumstances, but even if they are not, they will always act as though they were and even if they start with nothing, they often wind up very well off, due in part perhaps to this extremely positive attitude. They will always move with ease in high social circles. If there are good aspects to the Moon, they will have much good luck in life.

With this Moon there will be friendships with important and well-to-do people, especially women, who will help them achieve what they desire. Less evolved men with this position may tend to rely too much on the women in their lives to provide for them, while women with this Moon may be very shortsighted about the men they desire. This confident expectation of getting help whenever it is needed may go too far and become an attitude of "the world owes me a living." With the Moon in a fixed sign, some become pigheaded about going after what they want and may sacrifice many benefits in the process. They will ask and ask until the well runs dry before they realize that perhaps just wanting something isn't enough of a reason for getting it. They see themselves living in a certain pleasant fashion and may not care how they go about achieving it. Sometimes the warmth they project is only a ploy to get what they want. In these cases, there is usually a crisis that arises at some point in their lives to teach them true understanding.

These people have an easy and natural means of self-expression and are usually charming, knowing what to say to whom, and when, in order to get what they want. Those on a higher level will use their powers for the benefit of a group, raising funds, publicizing, or working in some way for a worthwhile cause. Those in public life will generally have some private cause to which they are devoted.

The Moon in the Twelfth House

This placement is similar in many ways to the Moon in the first house. People with the Moon in the twelfth are highly impressionable and sensitive; the mind floods with ideas and images and is open to inspiration. However, there is usually some constraint. Either they do not feel free for some reason to translate their inspirations and impressions into meaningful efforts, or these efforts meet with little or no success. The early life may be so turbulent with emotional crises of various kinds that they can't stick to anything long enough to bring it to completion. When there is success, it is often tinged with loneliness.

This is a rather lonely position in general. Men with this Moon placement often have a hard time maintaining a close relationship with a partner, or with anyone. If they do have a good relationship, the partner will often have to carry the burden of responsiveness as the man will cloak himself in self-isolation from time to time, and it will be up to the other to penetrate it. This usually comes from a painful relationship with the mother, the loss of the mother early in life, or the lack of her nurturing love.

Women with this position also find it hard to maintain a close and constant relationship over a long period of time. They have a great need for privacy. They are inclined to break off a relationship that threatens to become too intimate without explanation; to move, or take a job in another town and leave no forwarding address. Both sexes are often sentimental about love, but deep down they don't enjoy intimacy, and many times would rather do a disappearing act and keep the memories than go through the aches and pains of maintaining a long-term relationship.

This Moon gives deep insights into people and the truths that lie below the surface of appearances. It is good for creative efforts, especially the kind that are accomplished alone, or partly alone. There is an ability to appeal to an audience at a subliminal level. Often they cannot explain how they do it or even understand themselves why it works. This is a good position for detectives or for anyone who must seek answers below the surface. It is good for politicians because it gives the ability to appeal to the deeper needs of the public, although the public life may be marked in some way by tragedy or failure. They may have secret love affairs that bring sorrow or disgrace.

With a twelfth house Moon the public may be painful in some way. They may be excessively shy, suffer from claustrophobia, or have a fear of crowds. Their freedom may also be restricted in some way.

They do not like to be stuck in one place and will go from job to job until they find one in which there is a lot of mobility, where they must drive a lot, or can travel. If their job won't let them do this, they will save up for vacations in faraway places. They usually enjoy school, particularly the social aspect, and continue to learn and study one thing after another all their lives, though the formal side of learning, with its degrees and so on, is usually of little interest (unless the Sun or its dispositor is in Capricorn). They generally relate well to children and have a way with them. They keep a youthful, eager approach to life, and rarely get overweight or out of shape.

☿

Mercury Through the Houses

Mercury is the monitor of the energies of all the other planets, organizing and categorizing whatever comes to it. It is never more than thirty degrees from the Sun, and so it is always either in the same house as the Sun, or the one ahead, or the one behind. It is like a scout, riding in advance or to the rear of the Sun's energies and reporting back to it. Because it follows the Sun in its yearly round of the zodiac, Mercury takes about a year to complete its orbit.

Like the messenger god whose name it bears, Mercury is youthful, curious, eager, energetic, androgynous, tricky, loves motion, and desires to see everything and communicate everything it sees. It is closely related to youth and childhood, particularly the ages of four to fourteen, the years of learning by imitation. It is said to rule the "lower mind," that part of the mind that learns by rote, by imitation and memorization (rather than by deduction, reason, and conceptualizing, which are ruled by Uranus). Like the metal that bears its name, Mercury is volatile, bright, reflective, and cold. It rules the nervous system in the body, and the pineal gland in the brain, where the incoming data from sensory organs is monitored, categorized, and filed.

Mercury brings curiosity and a restless quality to the matters of the house where it is located. It assists the intuition in matters ruled by its house and sign. It works against emotional depth or display because its job is to learn as much as it can, remaining free to move on quickly to new things. For this reason, and because it is closely associated with youth, wherever it is located there is a tendency for the emotions to be superficial, childish, or imitative, particularly if it is closely allied in some way with one of the strongly emotional planets like the Moon, Neptune, or Venus.

Mercury on the angles gives the ability to learn quickly and to communicate well, and adds a youthful flair to the looks, style, and mannerisms, though it can also bring a nervous intensity that is very tiring. Mercury under the stress of bad aspects can indicate difficulties with the ability to learn or to communicate.

Mercury in the First House

This location of Mercury makes a good counselor. It is an excellent position for a teacher, actor, lawyer, politician, or anyone in similar careers as it gives the power to speak well, both to groups and in conversation. If there are limiting aspects from Saturn, or if Mercury is in a water sign, the ability to speak may be diminished, though the desire to communicate will be strong, and so may find an outlet through writing, singing, or film making, etc. In any case, people with a first house Mercury are almost always extremely quick, apt, flexible, and retain their youthful energy and enthusiasm throughout life.

Often they feel themselves to be the spokesman for a group and will feel called upon to speak out in defense of someone or something. They are usually witty (particularly if Mercury is in Virgo, Aries, or Gemini) and are able to use words to make others laugh. They are excellent teachers and, even if they don't teach as a profession, they will be useful throughout life instructing others, showing them how to do things.

They are able to put things into words much better than most people. Everything that they experience they frame in words or images, for themselves if not for others. If they can't put something into words or images it hardly exists for them. They are quick studies, able to pick up ideas rapidly from cursory reading or listening to others speak. They may become distracted by words or ideas, too caught up in them, if Mercury is in an air or earth sign. If it is in a water and fire sign, it is the thing itself they see, not the word for it, so this is a good position for an artist or poet who works more with images than with facts or concepts. Sometimes Mercury in a water sign even causes a problem with words.

They are often athletic, or physically active, loving motion and the use of their bodies as it is the sport itself, the game and the action, that they crave, and not so much the victory as this position is not competitive of itself. They are willing to take the less glorious roles in games or other group activities if the performance of the group as a whole requires it, as being part of the group or team is what appeals to them, although if they or anyone else appears to be treated unfairly they will not hesitate to speak out.

They either love speed or are insensitive to it and, if other factors are present, could have a car accident at some point due to their attraction to fast motion. They usually like the roller coaster and the faster, wilder rides at the amusement park. They usually love airplanes and flight, especially if Mercury is in a fire or air sign, and make good pilots.

If there are conjunctions or oppositions to Mercury from Saturn, Uranus, or Pluto, they may stammer or have a speech impediment, or possibly even brain damage. A retrograde Mercury may turn them towards writing, photography, art, or acting—anything where images or ideas can be constructed in private, because they may feel that the words they need to express themselves don't come easily enough in the spontaneous give and take of conversation.

If other chart factors are present that indicate long life, this position of Mercury strengthens them, giving a sort of perpetual youth and a strong ability to rejuvenate. However, if sudden death factors are present, this position will intensify those as well. In high political office it increases the potential for assassination. In some cases there is the possibility of an early death due in part to a distaste for aging.

Those with Mercury in the first house always relate well to young people and will have young friends even when they are old.

Mercury in the Second House

People with Mercury in the second house usually desire to be self-supporting early in life . They are always out to make a buck, and not always honorably or legally (the strength and elevation of Jupiter and Saturn will testify to this). They may live by their wits or by writing, speaking, acting, or teaching.

This location of Mercury contributes to sensuality and gives a strong interest in sex and a tendency to be attracted to more than one person at a time. At some time during the life there may be a powerful attraction to a much younger person. There is also a tendency to be attracted to socially inappropriate partners; in this, their desire to know and learn from what is opposite to the self taking a sexual form.

There is apt to be a stubbornness with this position; once the mind is made up it is hard to change it. This is even more likely if Mercury is in a fixed sign. There is a tendency (especially for those with the Sun in Virgo or Gemini) for ideas to crystallize, thus building a structure too rigid for a comfortable, free-flowing mental life. If this happens, events may occur at some point during the life that will be very painful as these crystallized ideas or attitudes are forcibly dissolved and restructured.

With Mercury in the second house the mind tends to work fairly slowly, one step at a time, and seeks to create a totally realistic, all-embracing, and dependable world view. Until this world view is complete (which is never), these people do not feel secure in venturing their opinions. They develop a philosophical nature: curious, eager to acquire facts, yet at the same time very slow to accept data that does not conform to their already crystallized ideas, and inclined to be less and less open as time goes by. They like to keep their ideas to themselves, and don't like to argue them out with others. They would sooner write a book or an article in which they can outline their entire view on a subject than discuss or argue it point by point with someone else. A free-flowing exchange on serious topics is uncomfortable for them, and they will usually shrug it off and back out rather than hash over a concept.

They tend to be quiet with strangers or in a group, though far from quiet at home or with intimates. They usually have good memories for facts, names, dates, places, and so on, which become etched in their minds, even if such details are not particularly useful.

Mercury in the Third House

This is an excellent position for a writer or communicator of any kind: filmmaker, photographer, graphic artist, secretary, lecturer, teacher. The mind is open and flexible, and keeps a youthful and eager approach to life, or at least to those areas of life on which it has decided to concentrate. There is a great interest in animals, children, and nature. There is an ability to move easily from one idea or field to another. With Mercury in fire or air, they are inclined to move too rapidly or easily, picking up nothing as they go, remembering little, and leaving no trace of having been there.

They usually have great stories about people they have known and places they have been. There is a great incoming stream of information about the world, but without aspects of crystallization these will form no philosophy or concepts, and will be put to no other use than amusing conversation with whoever is around. There is a great feel for the true sound and tempo of everyday life, that is good for playwrights, novelists, comedians, etc. It makes a person capable of being a very witty and entertaining companion. They usually have a wide circle of amusing acquaintances, although deep friendships must be shown by other factors.

They will gladly take the other side of the argument for the sheer pleasure of it and to keep up the excitement of a conversation, though they actually feel committed to no one position, which can be aggravating to those around them, who may feel that there is simply nothing there. They are better at providing a forum for others, recording others, helping others to bring forth their ideas, than they are at presenting their own, for often they have no real viewpoint, since they see so clearly all sides of a question.

They are resentful of pigeonholes and labels, love freedom and hate to be tied down, especially mentally (by a boring job or relationship). They will struggle until they find a spot where they can use their mentality as they please.

Mercury in the Fourth House

With this position of Mercury there is a great love of motion and travel, a great desire to see faraway places and to know exotic people, partly as a means for acquiring perspective on their own roots and early environment.

There may be a severing of ties with roots and early environment, and they may ultimately end up far from where they started. There may be quite a bit of travelling during childhood and the school years, with the family relocating a number of times.

Later in life, they may move away from their early roots and environment in a cultural as well as geographical sense, sometimes adopting a less civilized, less highly-educated, more basic lifestyle, or at least adopting its point of view, and working toward an understanding of such a lifestyle through writing, speaking, and so forth.

This position of Mercury is a partial testimony to a strong current of inner growth and self-development throughout life that takes them far from where they started in every sense, not just physically. There is often the lifelong styling of the self after an ideal and, consequently, a lifelong development along those lines, although it takes other factors to show what sort of an ideal not always a noble one.

These people have a very private mental life, and are highly individualistic in their way of thinking. They may have a rather lonely mental life and feel somewhat isolated, particularly in youth. The truth is that they are not afraid, as are most people, to think differently and willingly forge ahead along new lines of thought, taking each new idea and testing it, rejecting what doesn't fit their current system, yet basically maintaining a respect for all systems of thought. There is a lifelong search for a basic reality that can unite all disparate and seemingly opposing systems of thought, a search for what is basic to all of them. Ideas are loved, not for their intellectual patness, but for realism and practicality. There is usually an interest in history, anthropology, archaeology, as evidence of what has been, upon which their own personal world view can be based. The mind here is a digger, ever working down through facts toward fundamental truths rather than flying high after dreams and beautiful but insubstantial fantasies.

Those with a fourth house Mercury have an innate feeling for "the people," although they themselves generally remain aloof from large groups. They feel their own selfhood intensely, and it is hard for them to reach past it and touch the lives of others. It is often the sign of one who walks alone. They may become leaders if others urge leadership upon them, or they may shun it, but they will never be followers.

Mercury in the Fifth House

This position of Mercury is a powerful testimony to creativity. These are sturdy souls. They will never be downed by circumstance alone. In fact, they are often stimulated by difficulties to rise above them in a creative fashion, so they may actually seek trouble in some way so that this faculty will find expression, to the despair of less adventurous friends and relatives.

This Mercury adds flair to the style and charisma to the personality. They rarely look to others for answers. They have a deep belief in the creative powers of the self and are only too eager to use them. They must develop some area where this boldly innovative drive can be put to use or they will run headlong into difficulties with more conservative types. This is a very good position for artists, writers, lecturers, entertainers, etc. They do not work well in a career in harness with others, unless there is another area of the life where there is total working freedom.

Usually attractive physically, they may have a number of romances and affairs, though this energy is often translated into artistic efforts. If Mercury is near the sixth house cusp, there is also a tremendous capacity for hard work.

These people make excellent teachers. If they do not teach as a career—and bureaucratic constraints unfortunately often cause these naturally gifted teachers to flee the profession—they will somehow manage to arrange their lives so that they can do some teaching along the way. Children and young people are very important to them. If Mercury is under pressure from Mars, Saturn, or Uranus, parenthood may be denied, which will bring grief because they will be greatly desired. In this case, they will usually settle for adoption, or helping children or young people in some other way. They are usually attractive to children and younger people all their lives.

They are inclined to take chances and risks, drive fast, and race cars or horses, or at least admire those who do. They are romantics all their lives, scorning as dull the everyday routines that most people cling to.

Mercury in the Sixth House

With Mercury in the sixth there is a great need for meaningful employment. These individuals love to solve problems and will need a sphere in which problem-solving abilities are necessary. They will dive into work with tremendous intensity and enthusiasm, ignoring time and physical needs which will catch up with them later in symptoms of nerve strain and exhaustion.

If the ruler of the sign in which Mercury is located (its dispositor) is near an angle and is square or opposite the sixth house cusp, there may be some severe health problem at some time in their life, especially if a mutable sign is rising (Gemini, Virgo, Sagittarius, or Pisces). In this case they will struggle hard against the setback, either to overcome it, or to live with it and function in spite of it.

They are inclined to take themselves very seriously, and to be secretly afraid that others do not, although they may mask this fear behind self-deprecatory humor. If they have an easy manner it is usually affected, and not a reflection of their true nature, which is inclined to be intense.

With this position of Mercury the mind runs ahead of the body, forcing it to accomplish what the mind has conceived, and this can bring on exhaustion. They want to help solve the problems of humanity, and may work hard and selflessly toward this end. Their nerves are often working overtime, making it hard for them to relax. From time to time they may wind up in a state where they do not believe that they can accomplish physically what they see is necessary, which results in inertia. This inability to act is actually much harder on them than the strain of too much work.

Physical exercise is necessary for them to drain off their excess mental energy and keep it from affecting their physical system in a negative way. Since they are highly competitive in sports, for relaxation, they should choose something non-competitive, such as jogging or swimming.

They are hungry for appreciation, though often they do not show enough appreciation of others to warrant getting any themselves. They are usually too critical of themselves and must be constantly reminded that no one is or can be perfect.

Mercury in the Seventh House

Those with Mercury in the seventh have a great interest in people in general, and in what makes them tick. They want to experience the gamut of human relationships. Much here will depend on the aspects to Mercury. If trines and sextiles predominate, they will be the most pleasant and understanding of companions. With chiefly hard aspects, difficulties will be defined by the planets involved. Usually they are pleasant, even exciting, in one-to-one relationships. With oppositions, squares, and inconjuncts they may have trouble with the way they relate to groups. They may be paranoid, think too much about what others are doing or saying and worry too much about how they appear to others. They may originate rumors or stir up trouble, usually in an anxious effort to discover opinions about themselves.

This interest in people usually results in an understanding of others, not so much by empathy, which would require other aspects, as by knowing so many different types that repetitions are bound to occur, so that there finally develops a clinical knowledge of the ins and outs of the human psyche.

These people can't be accused of being locked up in themselves; if anything, perhaps of being locked out of themselves. They look to others in order to know and understand themselves. On the path to self-knowledge, they may give themselves over completely to a teacher at some point, or go from teacher to teacher, ever seeking self-revelation. They are not usually secure enough in their egos to seek the limelight.

They are usually restless, without as well as within, seeking an ideal place to dwell, and will travel a lot, or go from one living place to another. They may even try to change themselves totally in some way once or twice by moving away from home, changing their names, and so on.

They are not particularly faithful to mates, but if a mate leaves them, or is unfaithful, they will suffer agonies. They are forever seeking a place or a group that can reflect back a good image of the self. They may complain bitterly if things are not just right, yet they cannot bear to hear others complain.

Mercury in the Eighth House

This position of Mercury gives a deep, serious mentality, and although there may be the appearance of a breezy, easygoing nature, that is almost certainly a pose that has been adopted out of fear that the true nature, which is deeply serious, even solemn, will put others off.

These people may or may not be interested in money for its own sake, but they are usually very good at getting what they need when they need it. They generally know where to get the butter for their bread without necessarily working hard for it, and can't understand why others can't figure this out for themselves. This position often indicates an inheritance, although other factors will show if it is substantial and whether or not it will actually materialize.

These people may experience difficulty at some time during their lives over the question of their loyalty to some group. They may be put in a position where they will be asked to sell out, or choose one reality over another. They may or may not make the "right" choice, but the facts will be fully known only to themselves. Courage will always be needed with this position, although they may or may not rise to the need. There may be knowledge of other spheres of life that can show forth as religious faith, spiritualism, creative writing of the imaginative or fantastic sort, or psychic activity.

There is a constant awareness of mortality, and either courage and faith in an afterlife or a terrible fear of death. They may face death every day in some way, either by their own chronic illness or that of someone else who is close to them. They may have a job or career that involves risks, or working with other people who are at risk in some way, or death may haunt them simply because of their own paranoid fears.

If Mercury is under pressure from other planets, it can indicate a variety of mental problems, although great mental steadfastness under pressure is also possible. Once again, it is a question of rising to the occasion. There is also the possibility of the early death of a beloved younger person whose loss leaves them permanently changed somehow, either stronger and wiser or broken inside. Their own death is usually significant in some way, either by being dramatic, sudden, heroic, mysterious, or as the final act of a lifetime of courting death, or defying it.

This position of Mercury will contribute a certain charisma to the personality, making them attractive to others, although the nature of the attraction may be hard to define. It tends to give a pale or olive complexion, sometimes with many moles or freckles on the face. They are inclined to be thin, in youth at least.

They are drawn to extremes of style in speech, which can range from highly profane to affectations of breeding, street argot, unusually low or high pitch, or the vernacular of some group other than their own. There may be a stammer, which comes from a self-consciousness over revealing themselves through their speech. Sometimes, without realizing it, they will take on the persona of someone they admire; changing their role models and style as their interests evolve.

Mercury in the Ninth House

Here there is a great upward striving, especially when Mercury is in a fire, fixed, or earth sign. There is a desire to always appear at one's best, never to be outdone or made to look bad. Whatever storms may blow in these peoples' lives, they usually manage to land on their feet.

A ninth house Mercury often shows a rise in life through difficult circumstances, sometimes to considerable power. There is a mental restlessness with this position, a hunger for knowledge and experience that may lead to travel or long-term mental effort, some great study or piece of research or perfected virtuosity. There is also a loneliness here, the loneliness of the traveler, of the explorer. Actually, there is a need for aloneness, under the stars, alone with God, alone with Nature.

There is a need to experience the extremes of the human potential, to know how good one can be and how bad, how much one can learn about something, how much pain one can bear. This person will seek out friendships with those who have experienced all kinds of extremes. This is a very good position for ministers, and anyone with this Mercury will have moments when they will preach to anyone who will listen, about God, life, or other significant matters.

These people can be quite reckless. They are usually not afraid of dying, though they'd rather not, and will run risks in order to have deeply moving experiences. Women with this position have a royal bearing and great dignity. If Mercury is in Leo, they will rise to power if other aspects support it. If the mentality takes a religious turn, their upward striving may lead them away from the herd to holy places where they will strive to know God or be absorbed by nature. If not religious, they will be political, in which case they will work hard for a better society and for more personal power so that they can help change to come about.

If vilified, they will rarely stoop to defend themselves. They will speak out for causes, but about themselves they are usually silent. They will study and learn all their lives.

Mercury in the Tenth House

This position gives an extremely intense personality, particularly if Mercury is within five degrees of the Midheaven. These people are eager for the limelight, for recognition and praise. There is a great deal of pride in the self and the intellect, a great deal of ambition for mental achievement, to know a lot, to be able to speak well, always to know the right word, to express themselves accurately and with style. If Mercury is under pressure from hard aspects, there may be too much self-judgment; no achievement is great enough. They measure themselves against others they admire and often feel themselves lacking.

These people usually were encouraged to develop themselves early and were taken seriously during childhood by their parents (particularly their mothers), whose standards they may still use to judge themselves and others.

This is a good position for writers or actors. If Mercury is under pressure, there may be too much nerve activity for comfort. They may exhibit nervous habits, facial tics, etc. They may resort to drink or drugs to relieve the pressure on their nerves. They are "wired," tending naturally to be always on the updraft. Coffee or other stimulants are not good for them because they tend to be over-stimulated anyway.

They can get on talking jags that drive companions nuts, talking about themselves until everyone is exhausted, including themselves. They should be encouraged early to translate this self-awareness and communicativeness into acting or writing. This is hard for them unless they have a good strong Saturn because they tend to lack discipline. They respond so intensely to the stimulation of the passing moment that they are exhausted later and cannot harness their mental energies for long-term projects.

They are witty and clever with words, able to turn a phrase to amuse companions. They don't like to be alone and would much prefer to be surrounded at all times by exciting people. Nevertheless, it may be necessary for them to be alone from time to time for their mental and physical health, because company is so stimulating to them that they need the quiet of solitude to recharge their batteries.

They should be forewarned that their dreams of glory in youth must be exchanged for a more sober and down-to-earth view of reality, or they will awake in middle age to a life left in ruins by their pursuit of glory and excitement, at which point they may simply give up and die young of disillusionment.

Mercury in the Eleventh House

This location of Mercury strengthens the ego, making it easy to set long-term goals and stick to them. These people generally appear to be flexible and easy to get along with to those with whom they interact briefly, but over a length of time or from a distance it is apparent that they have been working inexorably towards personal goals all along. This says nothing of what kinds of goals they will choose; they may be the best possible or they may be totally irrational, linked to childhood fears, etc., but in either case, they will go after what they want until they get it, whether it is good for them or not. They will go through any number of horrific experiences, if necessary, in order to get what they want.

They are usually attractive, often with an electric quality to the personality that attracts others to them. Sometimes this electric quality is out in the open, blazing directly from their eyes; sometimes there is a veiled quality, as though masked, but waiting to blaze out.

Whatever their financial circumstances may be, they usually appear to others to be well off and to be able to get whatever they need whenever they want it.

They appear to be unconcerned with their own image, but actually they do care immensely how they look to others. They generally think quite well of themselves, and thus it is easy for them to create an exciting style.

They may be somewhat callous toward those nearest to them. They are more interested in their own feelings than they are in the feelings of others, and more interested in those who are interested in them than they are in those who aren't. They like to be at the center of an admiring group. However, much as they like others to be attracted to them, they are not deceived by flattery. They like to measure their effect on others by how many they can attract, yet they themselves will also be subject to powerful attractions to individuals or groups.

They are the busy bees of ideas, carrying them from one group to another, buzzing with excitement, pollinating the mind of humanity. Yet it is not really ideas that excite them; it is the people who have the ideas; or perhaps, in their eyes, these are one and the same.

Mercury in the Twelfth House

Individuals with Mercury in this position may have a damaged ego; if not, their ego has suffered in childhood from pressures that have toughened it. Their sense of self is often damaged in childhood, which can make them wary of exposing themselves and their feelings. They may even hide their own feelings from themselves, trying to be a different person from who they really are.

They are usually sensitive to the pain and trouble of others, though they may react in a variety of ways, one trying to help while another turns away. Some feel that they have such a hard time solving their own problems that they have no help to spare for others. If there are no other aspects or twelfth-house planets, they may try to help by preaching or lecturing, or by recounting what happened to them along the same lines, rather than by giving warmth, sympathy, or real assistance.

It is not a good position for self-acceptance. They are likely to spend a good deal of time fantasizing about themselves, refusing to face themselves squarely. It is hard for them to accept their own faults and weaknesses, and equally hard for them to believe in their own virtues and strengths. They often enjoy reading stories of other people, watching movies, plays, and so on, that give them the illusion of getting to know the truth about people. This is the soap opera position *par excellence.* They may even pry into the lives of others, looking for similarities to themselves, seeking justification for their own foibles (even, in extreme cases, watching people through binoculars, reading other people's mail, etc.). They are inclined to gossip about others. In most cases none of this is malicious, just the result of curiosity.

If they respond to this position at a higher level, they will want to understand themselves and will seek help from counselors, astrologers, psychiatrists, psychologists, psychics, or the like. They may study these subjects themselves in an effort to achieve more self-understanding, possibly even becoming practitioners.

This is a good position for a writer once the tendency to fantasize has been put into perspective. There is an instinctive quality to the mental processes. Sometimes they have trouble with straight facts, reacting better to the vibes in the air. They learn by absorbing ideas, not by study *per se*.

On the lower levels of response, they are inclined to overdo on eating, drinking, or drugs. Actually, sensible fasting is probably the best way for them to deal with problems.

They are inclined to be overly susceptible to praise, because they are so hungry for self-acceptance, and for the approval of others that will allow them to approve of themselves. If they rise to positions of power, they are apt to be led astray by flattery, if they are not careful.

♀

Venus Through the Houses

Venus is the harmonizer of the energies of the other planets, beautifying and polishing whatever comes its way. Its action is much like that of a handmaiden, always busy wherever it is, arranging, soothing, tidying, perfecting, and making the environment comfortable and beautiful. Venus rules love relationships as well as value systems.

Venus is never more than sixty degrees from the Sun, so it will either be in the same house (and sign) as the Sun or one or two houses in advance of it or behind it. Like Mercury, it follows the Sun in its orbit, and therefore takes an average of a year to complete its cycle through the zodiac.

Like the Roman goddess whose name it bears, Venus is the ruler of beauty and sensuality and has much to do with sexuality. In a chart, it has much to do with women, particularly women younger than the native. It is closely related to the years of awakening consciousness of sexuality and of the opposite sex, from age fourteen to twenty-one. It rules the skin and many of the glands throughout the body, particularly the endocrine system and the autonomic manufacture and release of the hormones that regulate the sex function, as well as other chemicals that regulate and balance other functions of the body. Its primary gift is that of balance, with all that implies—regulation, symmetry, perspective, moderate exercise, dance, and stories and songs that enable us to express our non-verbal feelings about things so that we can put them into perspective.

Venus enables us to finish things so that we can go on to other things. It works best in a secondary position, as a buffer to the more powerful energies of other planets. Where it is the most powerful it inclines to excess of partying, emotion, self-indulgence, and a love of luxury. It works subtly, by magnetism and secretion.

Venus on the angles adds intensity and charisma to the personality. There is a great hunger for love and approval, and a restlessness and courageousness in seeking it. There is also a hunger for beauty and for beautiful things (and people), and for the wherewithal to obtain them. It usually gives beauty, magnetic appeal, or both. Bad aspects to an angular Venus cause great unhappiness, and contentment is not likely, at least not in youth. However, it is a great stimulus to growth, because these people will be constantly seeking the happiness that seems to elude them. Many artists have created great works in the anguish of a badly aspected angular Venus; the oyster creating the pearl out of its agony.

In the fixed houses, Venus is more likely to be contented and stable, even with a difficult aspect or two, and is more likely to get what it wants. At the same time, it is less likely to create works of enduring value. Here it is more likely that life itself will be a work of art. If there are planets in trine, Venus can be lazy, taking what comes and making little effort to change. Glandular imbalances that cause physical imbalances, like weight problems and skin trouble, can often be traced to a Venus under stress.

Venus in the First House

A rising Venus gives beauty and charisma and the power to attract whatever and whomever is desired. The closer Venus is to the Ascendant, the greater is this power. This placement indicates at least one great love experience in the life, although the nature of that experience, whether happy or sad, short or long-lived, will be told by the sign Venus occupies, its relationship to its dispositor, and aspects from other planets.

These people have a great capacity to give love freely, unless Venus is in Capricorn, Aquarius, or Virgo, in which cases they are more reserved. Even so, their warmth comes through as interest in others, and may be intensified and refined by the restraint of these signs into a dispassionate love of humanity in general. In the first three signs, Aries, Taurus, and Gemini, Venus rising shows a great deal of self-love, though not necessarily the selfish kind that can't include love for others as well.

There is a strong potential for creativity with a rising Venus, but it requires other factors to put it to work. Usually, it shows more in the art of living than in works. These people are more apt to be great appreciators of the works of others, inspiring them with their enthusiasm and praise, by their beauty and style or, if they are well set financially, by their patronage and financial assistance.

Their good looks generally remain with them throughout life, and if Venus is in Virgo, Scorpio, Capricorn, or Aquarius, their looks often improve with age.

There is generally a good deal of sensuality with a rising Venus, that will be intensified or moderated by the sign Venus is in, by aspects from other planets, etc. The love of beauty extends to a love of sensual luxury, of satins and velvets, furs, delicious fragrances, perfumes, and jewelry. Companions may be chosen more for their physical beauty than the beauty of their souls. The closer Venus is to the second cusp the more pronounced the sensuality. If Venus is closely aspected by Uranus, Mars, or Pluto, has hard aspects and no easy ones, or is located in the twelfth house within ten degrees of the Ascendant, sensuality may bring sorrow. There may be scandal or grief in connection with love affairs or sex.

While the lives of those with a rising Venus may seem exciting and full of pleasure and variety to others, to themselves there is never enough. They are restless and eager for ever more varied and pleasurable excitement.

They have a great capacity for happiness and seek its source with unflagging energy, at least in youth, though the nature of the sources they seek will be different for each. There is always the danger of debauchery with a powerful angular Venus, and in the search for happiness they may have some degrading experiences. Neptune or Jupiter in square or opposition will show an inclination for too much partying. Nevertheless, Venus has the power to lead its followers out of any trouble it gets them into, and a rising Venus is a strong testimony to the ability to conquer problems like alcoholism or drug addiction. The urge towards happiness is so powerful that it can lead up as well as down.

If Venus is conjoined with other planets, the love nature will be modified accordingly. With Mars, there is a love of action or sports, with the passivity diminished. With Mercury, there is a love of motion or flight and an attraction toward younger people. With Jupiter, the love of good times, parties, elegant clothes and surroundings, beautiful people, and sensuality is intensified. Saturn here may exact too great a restraint unless there are compensating factors. With Uranus, expressions of love, beauty, and passion are alternately intensified and turned off, or sometimes intellectualized. With the Moon, a love of self, of women, and sensuality is increased. With Neptune, theatre, music and dance are emphasized, and, although sensuality is modified by romanticism, drugs and liquor are a real danger. With Pluto, danger is possible from sexual or romantic experiences.

A rising Venus indicates a great love of children and young people, particularly of girls.

Venus in the Second House

This is a powerful and secure location for Venus, because here it is in its native sector, sextile the Ascendant, and trine the Midheaven. Here it is able to govern the magnetic forces of the chart and gives the power to attract whatever is most desired: in earth signs, material things; in fire, thrills; in water, love and romance; and in air, friendships, contacts, and mental adventures.

A second house Venus does not necessarily show wealth, but without depressing factors, usually provides the resources to do whatever is desired at any given time. For those individuals who cannot provide for themselves for whatever reason, there will always be someone to turn to for help. In fact, this can indicate an overly-relaxed attitude towards finances ("the world owes me a living"), dulling the sense of need that spurs most people into gainful activity.

There is a strong sex drive that will pull them into one situation after another until it is satisfied. In Capricorn or Scorpio, there is a tendency toward homosexuality, or at least some homosexual experiences in the search for emotional fulfillment. In Aquarius, Gemini, Pisces, or Sagittarius, there is a tendency towards bisexuality or a lack of traditional sexual boundaries.

In Aries, there may be passionate sexual-romantic affairs, intense but short-lived. In Taurus, there will be life-long love relationships, with romantic beginnings and a strong sexual element. In Gemini, there may be friendships that turn into romances, and vice versa, with companionship always a big factor in any sexual relationship. In Cancer, deep emotional commitment is very important; there is also a passionate desire for children; the need for a partner to be parent to children is as or more important than the romantic element. A Cancer Venus here can't bear competition or jealousy and (particularly in a man's chart) may need mothering as much as sex, at least at the beginning.

In Leo, this Venus is intensely passionate; they need sex for release and tend to be faithful to one partner, but if the sexual relationship dies away they will find another somewhere else. In Virgo, Venus is faithful and shy, and works hard to establish a good relationship; they need partners who will build their confidence because they tend to be nervous, and may need to practice relaxation techniques to fully enjoy sex. With Venus in Libra, the attractiveness of the partner is extremely important; they tend to be faithful, but can be enticed from time to time by passing romantic attractions. Venus in Scorpio is passionate and jealous, with periodic upheavals in the sex life due to jealousy. In Sagittarius, Venus is more interested in novelty and change, or in the personality, importance, or exotic qualities of their partners than in the quality of the sex relationship. Venus in Aquarius in the second house is a strong testimony for homosexual (or asexual) relationships, the desire being more for intellectual companionship, with less concern for sexual compatibility, and sometimes even a dislike of physical sex. In Pisces, there is a great need for tenderness and emotional rapport; without this, the sex life will not develop but will remain on a fantasy level.

Venus in the Third House

This placement of Venus gives the ability to communicate ideas through a variety of means and forms. It gives a love of ideas for their own sake and, with Mars contacts, a willingness to argue or fight for them.

The love of ideas may interfere with the ability to fully experience love itself. This mental aspect to the Ascendant (thirty degrees) isn't really the perfect spot for the true nature of Venus to manifest at its best. Venus' power is to relax tension so that beauty and happiness can be experienced fully. The vibratory level isn't right at this angle, so these people often let their thoughts and ideas get in the way of the comfortable intimacy and long-term love relationships that are the promise of Venus at her best. There is almost always a certain amount of frustration involved in love relationships with this position, and it is a partial testimony against marriage. This is just as well, for when they marry they often do so for the wrong reasons, so the marriage won't last or isn't happy.

These people are usually extremely creative and, given more testimonies, should concern themselves more with establishing a career than with marriage and family. Once they are well on their way to making a name for themselves in their chosen field, it will become evident whether or not marriage and children will fit into their way of life. The offspring they will leave to posterity are very often "brain children"; works of art and ideas that are very difficult to produce along with the flesh and blood article. They are usually fond of children, but are often quite content to play the role of uncle, aunt, god-parent, and so on to the children of their relatives and friends. They need affection just as much as anyone, but what they don't need is the constant pressure of demands on time and emotion that drains them of the energy and time they need to get things—their things—accomplished. Usually, there is a strong lifelong relationship with one or more siblings, neighbors, or friends, and it is often through sharing these lives from the sidelines that this position achieves its richest emotional fulfillment. Venus at this angle is very suscepti-ble to difficulties from tension-producing aspects and, where this is true, there may be a good deal of suffer-ing connected with these relationships.

They usually love speed and vehicles that can give them the thrill of rapid motion. They may also love horses and riding. If Venus is squared or opposed by Mars or Uranus, there may be the possibility of acci-dents (if squared and/or opposed by *both* the rulers of the eighth and first houses, potentially fatal).

These people are usually attractive to others, but often present a cool or unconcerned exterior, one that is not openly warm or inviting. They may be rather abrupt or disconcerting in their mode of speech or behavior towards those who don't know them well.

The Greek myth of Cupid and Psyche illustrates the difficulties of the planet of love in this mental house. The curiosity (intellect) of Psyche (the subconscious mind) overcomes her vow to her husband Cupid, the god of love, who always comes to her under cover of darkness, that she will not look at him or try to discover his real name; and so she loses him. This myth illustrates what happens when the mind oversteps its natural boundaries and becomes too concerned with the sources and mechanisms of passion.

Venus in the Fourth House

With good aspects, this is a good place for Venus. There will be great pleasure in the home, much love and sharing. There is a love of family and of family tradition, an interest in roots and heritage, which may include history, wealth, nobility, things in which we can take pride. The father is usually handsome, charming, easy-going, or fun-loving. It is a partial testimony to daughters, sisters, and female relatives, usually attractive, fun-loving and artistic.

The home environment is very important to these people, who will be inclined to spend a large portion of the money available to them on it, painting, cleaning, restoring, adding on, and renewing. They are more inclined to enjoy staying home or entertaining at home than going out. They may even have a business in their home, a workshop, or work out of their home in some way. It is a partial testimony to success in real estate, landscaping, gardening, or inn-keeping.

Without stress aspects, it indicates a happy childhood with indulgent parents and a peaceful, happy old age.

With difficult aspects, however, this house is not such a good place for Venus. The angularity is intense, so that difficulties are magnified. The early environment may be pleasurable or exciting in some way, but too hectic, confused, or unstable. The father may be not only indulgent, but self-indulgent as well, and get into financial difficulties. He may be too fun-loving, drink, or have affairs. Either the childhood home or the father (or both) may be lost, leaving a bittersweet memory of a time and place that is gone forever. A self-indulgent mother may dominate the home environment.

In any case, whatever problems this angular Venus may bring with hard aspects, it generally forces them to rebuild their personal set of values from the ground up. Something is wrong with the value system inherited from the family, and they must reexamine everything in light of personal experience and study in order to reevaluate goals, lifestyle, and basic attitudes. A stressed fourth house Venus forces one to grow and keep growing throughout life. At first there may be some unfortunate experiences, but, as they live and learn, they pass through many stages and come at last to a much better understanding of life. It is a strong testimony for wisdom in old age, however painful or pleasant the means of acquiring it, and for the contentment that wisdom brings.

Venus in the Fifth House

This is an excellent location for Venus. Almost always with this location there is a great outpouring of creative energy throughout the life. It takes a barricade of terrible aspects to block the glow of life-giving and life-loving energy maintained by this angle of Venus, 120 degrees from both Ascendant and Midheaven. These people find it easy to express themselves without restraint by whatever means are at hand. The worst stress aspects only seem to increase their powers.

This is a good position for an athlete because it is highly competitive and eager for contest and victory, though it is not so good for a team player as they aren't willing to take a secondary position for long. It is also a good position for teachers, the creative drive here being used to catch the imagination of the students.

Romance is very important to these people; they will marry only for love. Romantic love is a god to them, and they will want to sacrifice much for it at one time or another, though they may refrain out of loyalty to the emotional status quo, which is also very strong. They know their own creative strength comes from the loving approval of those around them, and so do not want to kill the goose that lays the golden egg.

They are kind, thoughtful, and considerate when Venus is in an air sign, passionate in when it is in a fire sign, sentimental when it is in a in water sign, and unshakable in when it is in an earth sign. They are extremely generous of self and goods, unless their passion goes elsewhere, though loyalty will maintain a dribble until the end.

They are good farmers and gardeners; their creative energy gives them a green thumb and plants seem to spring up in their presence. They are eager to be parents, but if this fate blocks this somehow, they will usually find some way to work with children as their instinct is so strong; or if not children, animals.

They are very hard workers at what they enjoy, but lazy about doing anything else, feeling no tremors of insecurity as they wait for their luck to come along, which it always does. They have a tremendous amount of physical energy at their disposal, which helps in a career of sports or dance (or anything, really). This gives the energy to embark upon a career, but often diminishes the follow-through; as these people must follow their own growth, and so often make mid-life changes that can hurt a lifetime career thrust. Usually, they are more interested in doing whatever excites them at the moment than in maintaining any kind of long-term career commitment, although if tenth house planets and other factors testify to a career, this will certainly strengthen it.

They are usually enthusiastic about food, cooking, and eating, and are good cooks, often combining gardening and cooking into a search for the perfect dining experience.

Venus in the Sixth House

These people love to work, and work at love. Frequently, a romantic attraction tempts them into a job situation, or they are attracted to a field of endeavor more by the practitioners than by the work itself. Throughout life they are prone to on-the-job romances, and may marry someone they meet on the job. They may become involved in the theater, films, photography, modeling, magazines, or any of the so-called glamour industries (advertising, TV, radio, etc.).

They will rarely last long on a job they don't like, and will soon find the kind of work that makes them happy.

They are capable of giving their all to a job they do like, and frequently do not get the recognition they deserve since seeing the job well done is their primary interest. The only danger here is that they do not always examine the long term or overall effects of their efforts.

This Venus is a difficult position for romance, and most with Venus here will have at least one major heartbreak in their lives. Sometimes their workaholic attitude is a substitute for the true love they think they cannot attract, a means of getting the praise and response they think they can't get from lovers. (The closer Venus is to the descendent the less this is likely to be an issue.)

They may be very attractive, but unfortunately never as attractive as they'd like to be. If there are bad aspects to the Moon, they may have skin trouble or difficulties with the endocrine or lymph systems, all of it emotional in origin. Anyone with a sixth-house Venus needs some kind of daily physical regimen to stay healthy mentally, physically, and emotionally. Usually, though, they are quite health-minded and take good care of their bodies.

This is a good placement for a doctor or a nurse or anyone working in the health care sector. It's also good for musicians, or athletes, those who must drive themselves towards perfect performance through a daily practice of skills.

Venus in the Seventh House

These people are always attractive, exuding warmth, charm, and exciting vivacity. The truth is that they are highly stimulated by the presence of others, so this is how they always seem when others are at hand to take notice. They generally marry early and rarely refrain from marriage, or at least from mating, because they are drawn into unions with others, sometimes almost against their will. In cardinal or mutable signs there may be more than one marriage, certainly more than one relationship. It may seem to them that others force themselves upon them, yet it is they who attract others by the intensity of their response.

Males with this aspect may get involved in homosexual relationships early in life. It is a partial testimony to homosexuality in either male or female charts, or a sexual ambiguity or bisexuality, because they find it hard to resist whatever comes to them.

Later in life, they will be attracted to those younger than themselves, and they always respond to children. (Only with seriously bad aspects is there the danger of inappropriate sexual behavior with children.) It is a good position for parents and teachers because the loving Venusian energy will have a natural and needed outlet on a regular basis, and so won't get dammed up, possibly causing a social catastrophe when it bursts out.

The closer to the eighth house cusp, the more sexual the energy becomes, and the more intense the powers of physical attraction. In Aries, there will be many brief sex contacts throughout life, possibly beginning very young. In Taurus, it indicates early marriage, usually faithful, but, even so, times of great temptation; in Gemini, many relationships, and likely more than one marriage. In Cancer, the Moon sign will determine the effect. If it is in Virgo or Capricorn, the individual will be a late bloomer, attractive into later life. Venus in Scorpio, Taurus, or Leo, can be result in a sexual guru who attracts a train of followers through charisma; usually to no good end.

Venus in the seventh is a good position for an actor, performer, writer, or politician, as the attraction enhances their performance and ensures a willing audience. It is not good for ministers; the sexual charisma, while attracting a following, is too likely to result in scandal.

Venus in the Eighth House

Here, Venus gives a charisma that outshines any physical imperfections, attracting others in a singular manner that is hard to define. There will be a great test of loyalty at some time during the life, requiring some kind of sacrifice. If there are oppositions or inconjuncts to Venus, this may be a great sacrifice, such as the physical relationship with the beloved.

Love is always bound up with death, loyalty, and sacrifice in some way. It is likely that they will suffer the death or permanent loss of someone beloved, someone beautiful and good. This loss, and its inherent threat of further loss, permanently affects their outlook on life. If the Sun is also in the eighth house, their entire life may be bound up in a drama of love, loyalty, and sacrifice, with death as the last act. This is an extremely self-sacrificial position.

These people take themselves very seriously. They don't wear their hearts on their sleeves and are very cautious about giving their affections, because any mistake in this area will leave them shattered. They suffer so from unrequited love that they are extremely cautious, and will wait for a long time before declaring themselves, but once they give their hearts it is usually forever.

They love stories of romantic courage, loyalty, and sacrifice. If they are artists, their works have the same appeal that their personalities have, a sort of pathos, tenderness, and idealism at the heart of a bitter and ironic realism. They are both idealist and cynic, romantic and realist, and the excitement of their personality comes from a constant tension between these extremes.

This position testifies to one whose feelings were persistently ignored or badly hurt in childhood, so that they remain cautious throughout life. If they attain power, they may be cold or cruel to others who they imagine might be cold or cruel to them, though they are usually extremely sensitive and tender toward children, the disabled, animals, or anyone who is clearly vulnerable and from whom they can feel no potential threat.

They are very sexual and love to make love, but are capable of great restraint. They tend to be jealous, but if forgiveness is asked, will give it freely.

Venus in the Ninth and Tenth Houses

Here we see the power of love versus the love of power. Venus at the top of the chart gives good looks and, frequently, real beauty, but in any case there is always the ability to command attention.

Many monarchs, politicians, and statesmen have Venus near the Midheaven. It is a particularly good position for those interested in a career in the arts, though it is good for any career as it attracts favorable attention. If they become public figures, the public is inclined to love them and to forgive all faults. The public will be very interested in their love lives because they will always appear to be surrounded by romantic intrigue. The public is inclined to make them into icons or institutions in later life, and enshrine them after death as symbols of something. This will be true to a lesser extent even for those who never reach beyond smaller circles, since they will still be known by name by more people than they know personally, and their lives and loves will be discussed and wondered at by the community at large.

They are excellent salesmen, but their most important product is themselves. They are usually extremely adventurous and love travel and motion, finding it very heard to stay put for any length of time. If career or family demands keep them in one place, they will take vacations to distant places.

They are fascinated by faraway places and far-out ideas, yet usually remain attracted to conservative values and to the friends and scenes of their youth. They may suffer stress from being torn between new ideas and their promoters and the old tried and true, never really able to give up the latter. For some reason, Venus at the Midheaven gives tremendous physical stamina and courage and the urge to conquer the heights, literally—manifested in a love of mountains and the grandeur of Nature.

With Venus in the ninth on the cusp of the tenth, they tend to back causes; in the tenth, their big cause is themselves. In the ninth, this is an achiever who never stops trying, with a love of philosophy and travel; in the tenth there is tremendous personal authority. Many generals have Venus in the tenth. In either house they are great intriguers, diplomats, and manipulators.

They are inclined to be narcissistic, more interested in themselves and their own ideas and needs than in those of others, but they are so attractive that no one minds. They are inclined to go their own way, and others can follow if they choose, which they usually do. They are extremely adept at getting their own way.

If there are bad aspects to Venus there may be a weight problem, emotional in origin. A fear of sex could be the root cause of this, particularly with women, who may overeat to fill a hunger for love. They may also turn gray early in life. They may experience difficulties having children; love affairs or children may be destructive or tormenting. With bad aspects to Venus at the Midheaven, there is always danger of a sex scandal at some time in the life.

They are inclined toward luxury and they love to surround themselves with objects of beauty, both animate and inanimate. They have a great appetite for grandeur, and will go to it (the mountains) or build it around themselves (Versailles).

Venus in the Eleventh House

People with Venus in the eleventh house are dreamers, weavers of fantasies, eloquent speakers, and good storytellers. They have elegant manners and move through the crowd with cheerful authority. They exude confidence in speech and manner, and act as though born to the purple, with an air of casual elegance that others seek to emulate. Frequently they are inheritors of wealth and position, but, if not, they have the opportunity to observe those who are, and learn their style and manner.

They are extremely inventive, and their active imaginations are put to use inventing anything from get-rich-quick schemes to science fiction to more or less useful and lucrative inventions.

They have pleasant, mellow voices and are usually good singers, able to accompany themselves on a piano or guitar and to amuse themselves and their companions without a whole lot of effort or training. They love to party and hang out, which, with other party-hearty aspects, can get to be too much of a good thing.

This is a good position in any chart because it assures a certain amount of success in almost any endeavor and the granting of at least one major wish. However, without an iron will (strong Sun, Mars, Saturn, or Pluto aspects) there is the danger of resting too long on the laurels, of drifting with pleasing circumstance with little effort beyond what is necessary just to keep floating along. A strong Mars is needed and a well-placed Saturn or Uranus for these people to mobilize their energies, from merely enhancing the passing moment, into something more permanent. Without pressure aspects, they have a tendency to live in their dreams and imaginations while doing their best to steer clear of cold hard reality. It is too bad if they do, because any effort on their part will bring results unusually quickly.

This position of Venus doesn't modify stronger and more ambitious aspects and locations, but it adds a veneer of *bonhomie,* of good fellowship and charm, that can hide an iron will, if it is there, and create the illusion that the climb to the top has been without effort.

They always benefit greatly from the admiration and assistance of women and young people of wealth and position. As for a career, these people can benefit more from a round of parties than most can from months or even years of hard work.

Venus in the Twelfth House

Here matters ruled by Venus will bring sorrow in some form. Those benefits brought by the other houses are either denied or overdone, depending on the aspects to Venus (oppositions and inconjuncts deny, everything else overdoes). The search for love and pleasure can go to extremes, bringing scandal, sorrow, health problems, and, if Mars or Uranus is aspected, violence and trouble with the law.

People with this location of Venus must learn to approach love, sex, and partying with extreme caution, because these pleasures have a way of turning around on them, causing a great deal of grief and trouble. Their hearts will be broken by sad love affairs, or a secret love must remain hidden for many years, or there will be something that gives them an excuse to give way to drinking out of self-pity. They are inclined to get involved with the wrong people or give their affections to someone who is bad for them. Location in the sexually oriented signs with bad aspects to Saturn, Pluto, and Uranus could indicate promiscuity, sexual perversion, sadomasochism, venereal disease, or sexual abuse in childhood or youth. This is frequently the sign of the abused or neglected child, still seeking compensation in adult life for what was lacking in childhood, and, with bad aspects, wreaking vengeance on a world felt to be cold, cruel, and rejecting.

With strong supportive aspects and a generally well-balanced chart, these difficulties may manifest chiefly in youth, maturity bringing self-knowledge, inner healing, and wisdom. Even so, matters of the heart will always be problematic. The best use of Venus in the twelfth is to direct the love nature towards helping those less fortunate, although healing society at large cannot truly compensate for a lack of healing within.

This is an excellent position for fiction writers as writing fiction can provide a harmless outlet for these turbulent energies, perhaps even a means of harnessing them for profit.

The closer Venus is to the ascendant, the more attractive they will be, and the more frequent, intense, and outward the romantic and sexual events of the life will be, but as long as Venus is in the twelfth, it will bring problems.

The Sun Through the Houses

The location of the Sun by sign determines the basis of what most people know about astrology—the Sun sign, or "what we are," and although astrologers condemn this as gross oversimplification, it does point out the power of the Sun's location in the chart. After all, the Sun, though called a planet in astrology for the sake of simplicity, is, in reality, a star, and the center of the system of planets of which the Earth is but one, their primary source of life and energy. Therefore, it is understandable that the location of the Sun is one of the most important factors in a chart, if not *the* most important. We define our year by the amount of time it takes the Sun to circle the zodiac.

The sign location of the Sun is the most easily determined factor in a chart because it can be figured immediately from the month and day of birth, but its *house location*, which can only be figured from an ephemeris, is just as important to the understanding of a person's nature as its sign location. In each of the twelve signs, the Sun's energy is temporized by the nature of the sign, except in the sign Leo, always considered the Sun's best location, where it is free to manifest unmodified by a *dispositor* (the planet that rules the sign where a planet is located). In every sign but Leo, the Sun's dispositor shares the second most important position in a chart with the planet that rules the sign on the Ascendant, and with a rising planet, if there is one. Thus, the relationship, by aspect, between the Sun and its dispositor is one of the most important considerations in delineating a horoscope.

The Sun is too powerful to be limited by location in a weak sign or house; it brings its strength wherever it goes. The same is true for its relationships with the other planets; it lends them its strength and can work equally well with all of them. However, problems can arise through aspects to the Sun. Planets in opposition are at a great disadvantage and will create a great deal of stress during transits. The only situation that can really weaken the Sun in a chart is having no aspects to it at all. This reflects a life that is out of touch with its own center.

The Sun is thought to rule the constitutional health (as opposed to the periodic health, which is ruled by the Moon). Stressful aspects to the Sun can cause chronic illness, while stresses to the Moon cause briefer and lesser physical problems. In the body, the Sun rules the center of the torso and most of the organs in that area from the heart to the solar plexus, some elements of the blood, and the amount and kind of basic energy that keeps the organism functioning. For instance, the Sun in Gemini guarantees a plentiful supply of mental energy, but unless Mars is in a fire or earth sign, physical energy may be in short supply.

The Sun is said to rule the years between "coming of age," from age twenty-one to around thirty-five, when humans are first experiencing and getting used to independence and self-determination. These are years of expansion, of learning by trial and error, when the ego is fresh and strong and not yet humbled by weight of years, when lifelong responsibilities are taken on lightly, without forethought.

The Sun is said to rule the ego, one's sense of self. Therefore, its location by sign and house says much about a person's idea of themselves. It also tells much about the men in a person's life, especially the father, and in a woman's chart, her husband and/or lovers.

The Sun in the First House

This is a powerful location for the Sun. It gives great strength, a strong ego, and physical stamina. People with with a rising Sun are inclined to be self-indulgent. They go after what they want without a second thought, and usually get it. They tend to be autocratic with children, employees, and hangers-on, but are also generous in a patriarchal way. They are usually attractive, with an air of aristocratic authority or dignity. Their strong egos make enemies, whom they generally ignore. If Mars, Uranus, Saturn, or Pluto are conjunct or square the Sun, they can be cruel, but usually they are kind, generous, and paternalistic to others. That is, unless their anger is aroused or their status is threatened, when they can become extremely dangerous to any they perceive as a threat. When they fight, it is animalistic, no holds barred—and they usually win.

They may be lazy, unless they are working toward something they really want or care about, in which case their strength and energy are double that of anyone else. They rarely pursue anyone; usually they don't have to, as they attract others easily and will take their pick of friends and lovers from among those who come to them. When friends become disenchanted by their lack of interest in anyone but themselves, they do not suffer over the loss but simply turn to someone new. It is a good position for leaders who must pull others with them, such as politicians, performers, and statesmen, because the charisma here extends well beyond their immediate circle to those who know nothing of their personal lives.

The Sun rising gives great strength and vitality, but takes away sensitivity and insight into others. Even if the Sun is in a water or air sign, everything must be related to the self before it can be accepted. This is a powerful position, but inclined to be narrow in perception. Other aspects can broaden the perspective, but nothing can mitigate the intense egoism of this position. They can be incredible liars, but their lies are the truth to them. They structure reality to suit their needs, rather than the other way around. They can usually make a convincing case for black being white, and vice versa.

It is a difficult aspect for marriage for a woman. She may appear passive in the beginning, but her need to dominate will surface sooner or later, and then, husband beware! She needs her own arena in which to become important or she will try to take over his.

The rising Sun gives a strong constitution which can take a lot of punishment in every way and come back for more. They are usually extremely healthy, though there is a danger of fevers and accidents, especially in youth, and sometimes heart trouble later in life.

The Sun in the Second House

With the Sun here there is instinctive good taste, with a feeling for the basic worth of things and the ability to translate this awareness into dollars and cents. There is a need to be surrounded by beauty and quality. These people are strongly attracted to those who can provide them with the environment they seek. Generally "handy," they are able to create attractive environments, so this is a good position for architects, builders, carpenters, landscapers, and interior decorators, as well as fashion designers, dressmakers, hair stylists, jewelers, perfume and cosmetics manufacturers, and all those who are adept at enhancing the environment or the body.

Very sensual, they have a powerful sexual charisma that enables them to attract others easily. They are usually quite successful at establishing sexual relationships with those they desire. If other aspects frustrate this, it can be a source of great physical and emotional suffering because the desire nature is so powerful. It is very important that there be sufficient love from both parents in infancy and childhood. Otherwise, the need for it may manifest later in agonizing desires and abnormal sex relationships. The stability of a dependable on-going sexual relationship is a real need. They will work hard at a marriage because of this. Separation and divorce only occur when the sexual aspect of the relationship fails.

The desire to be independent of others is a powerful motivating force that can result in success. It can also create difficulties by keeping them from joining partnerships, groups, companies, staffs, or other organizations that are necessary to establish any kind of work/career position in the community. Most women, and some men, with this Sun position are into body culture in some way, frequently dancing, or, if the Sun is in a water sign, swimming.

The Sun in the Third House

The Sun at this communicative angle is an excellent position for teachers, writers, actors, performers of any kind, or for any position in television, film, advertising, publishing, or communications. They have a facility for transmitting information, ideas, and new ways of looking at things.

Good companions, they usually have a wide circle of friends and acquaintances. They usually have at least one brother who is important to them. If not, establishing a permanent brotherly relationship with a male friend is very necessary. They are good neighbors (unless there are afflictions) and usually work to keep up relationships with friends, family, and neighbors, organizing get-togethers, relaying news, and so on. If they get into politics, it is usually more because some group needs a spokesman than because of their own hunger for power or the spotlight.

They don't like to be stuck in one place and will go from job to job until they find one that offers a lot of mobility; for instance, where they must drive a lot or can travel. If their job won't let them do this, they will save up for vacations in far-away places.

They usually enjoy school—particularly the social aspect—and continue the study of one thing after another all their lives, though the credit aspect, degrees, etc., is usually of little interest (unless the Sun or its dispositor is in Capricorn). They generally relate well to children and have a way with them. They maintain a youthful, eager approach to life, and rarely get overweight or out of shape.

The Sun in the Fourth House

Deeply concerned with basic values, these people generally have a philosophy of life that makes them uncomfortable with mere surface show. They crave to live righteously, to be a meaningful part of a healthy society. They will work hard to own their own home or a piece of land. If they grow up in comfortable surroundings, they may find it hard to leave. They usually stay near their childhood roots, maintaining the family and neighbor relationships they have known since childhood. If life forces them out and they must live far from "home," they will miss it, sentimentalize it, and yearn for it.

They gravitate toward the kind of work they can do at home; if they must have an office or place of business away from home, they will usually contrive to do their creative thinking at home.

Politically they seek a just society, with equal opportunity for all. To this end they will work hard, usually on the thankless, organizing, detail end. They tend to shun the limelight and, when they must step forward, are known for their modesty and concern for issues rather than ego.

They tend to be shy and undemonstrative (unless other aspects contradict), but their feelings are deep and active and they never forget love or kindness. They have great endurance, usually work into old age and, if forced to retire, soon find something useful to keep them active.

The Sun in the Fifth House

Those with Sun in the fifth possess a strong sense of self, a natural pride and dignity, and exhibit great creativity and originality in everything they do. They can be self-centered, so inner-directed that they may lose sight of others, but once reminded, are usually quick and generous in their response. They like being left alone to do things their own way, though, as soon as they feel the need for companionship, it is easy for them to find, as they are charming and entertaining companions.

They are usually healthy, strong, and very courageous—physically in earth, mentally in air, emotionally in water; and apt to be reckless in fire, taking risks without paying much attention to danger.

They are very inclined toward love affairs and romance all their lives which can be a problem; other aspects will show how much of a problem. Affairs are brief, intense, and sexual in Aries; they are sexual and enduring in Taurus, and liable to become marriages or as enduring as marriages. In Gemini, affairs will be sentimental or mostly mental; they may involve two partners at once, or a relative, neighbor, or childhood companion. In Cancer, love affairs are very emotional; in Leo, very sexual; in Virgo, cautious but enduring; in Libra, marriage, sometimes several, sometimes a refusal to marry anyone; in Sagittarius, intense but brief; in Capricorn, slow to develop but enduring; in Aquarius, either sudden and unique, or similar to Capricorn; in Pisces, sentimental first, then sexual.

There is a danger with this fifth-house Sun of withdrawing from life to too great an extent, shutting out the world and its confusing demands, protecting a privacy that becomes all-engulfing, particularly later in life. Here are mavericks, eccentrics, loners; those who go their own way, no matter what. There is the danger of ignoring the attitudes of society to too great an extent, ignoring public opinion.

These people are hard workers, able to keep at the job longer than others. They like to work hard and relax thoroughly. Physically, they are healthy and strong. They generally like competitive sports, especially in earth and water signs, and like to play hard to use up their abundance of physical energy. The competitive nature of the fifth house is not so apparent with the Sun in it; it seems to scorn competition. The true competition here is with the self, to outdo oneself, to be better each time than the time before. Self-development is generally more important than a single steady career effort.

Frequently, the family pet in childhood, the apple of their parents' eyes, these individuals have been given such a strong sense of their own innate worth and importance that they feel no need to prove themselves to anyone but themselves.

The Sun in the Sixth House

This can be an awkward placement for the Sun unless it is supported by strong aspects from other planets. This is "Saturday's child" who must work for a living. Generally not the family pet, they were loved, perhaps, but not enough. They must get away from the home environment in order to discover their worth among strangers. At home, they may crave the love of a parent, particularly the father, and see all of it go to a brother or sister instead.

Away from home, they still have a hard time fitting in and often feel somewhat out of place or misunderstood. Their egos are not strong with the sun at this 150 degree angle of sacrifice, and they need a good deal of stroking by those who love them, though they will rarely ask. They are hard workers, very demanding of themselves and of others who may work for them. They yearn for the perfect work situation, with a boss who behaves like a good father—demanding, yet understanding and appreciative—though few find it.

Disgust over bad work situations often drives them to work on their own, yet this is not the answer, either. There is a loneliness here, a feeling of being off to one side, unrecognized. They do best in the helping professions, as doctors, nurses, veterinarians, social workers, healers, special education teachers, or working with the underprivileged or handicapped. They can identify with those they serve, to some extent, and their need to lose themselves in work goes for a clearly recognized cause and is of obvious value. Their need for love and appreciation, if unrecognized or unfulfilled, can manifest physically as a variety of illnesses or psychological problems.

If the Sun is trine the Midheaven or if another important planet is in the tenth house, there may be an opportunity to rise past all difficulties by means of a successful career effort.

The Sun in the Seventh House

"Always true to you, dear, in my fashion; always true to you, darling, in my way."

This is a strong position for the Sun, bringing all the qualities that come with an angular Sun; strong sense of self, strong constitution, powerful will, but at this 180 degree angle, these people always need partners in order to put their tremendous capabilities to work. Until they have found the appropriate partner, they will seem to drift from one thing to another. This is true of love partners as well as business or professional partners. Those with the Sun in a fixed sign, no other planets in the seventh house, and no unrelieved afflictions, will probably take their time about finding a partner and then remain with the same person for life. Such people are inclined to be somewhat emotionally dependent and, if the partner breaks off the relationship, leaves, or dies, may feel that their lives are shattered.

Those with the Sun in cardinal or mutable signs, or with other planets in the seventh, are not likely to remain with one partner, and some will change partners regularly throughout long, lusty lives, perhaps even maintaining several long-term relationships at once. Their need for a partner usually finds them married at a very early age and, as an angular Sun is a sign of life-long growth and development, they often outgrow these early relationships and move on to greater challenges in their love lives as their capacities grow. They usually have a philosophy of life that suits their style and needs, and so will be advocates of free love, open marriage, or something of the sort—privately if not publicly.

As long as they have a dependable partner, these people can support whole tribes of admirers, dependents, employees, and such, standing gladly at the center of movements, special interest groups, cults, etc., as a father or mother figure. They have a great sense of purpose and make good leaders, but whether for good or evil must be indicated by other factors, as their sense of being right is so strong that they can take large numbers of their fellows a long way down the wrong path.

Although this is a strong location for the Sun, it is not so good for a career, as they are so strongly inclined to follow their own private star wherever it may lead. The path of personal development will carry them far from a single career track, and they may end up a long way from where they began.

The Sun in the Eighth House

Here the Sun gives strength, independence, endurance, and great potential power, which can show forth in the outside world as success in business, politics, the arts, or in any arena. There is the ability to sense what will work and the courage to act on it. There is also an ability to manage others with skill, though that skill may sometimes appear somewhat Machiavellian.

Unfortunately, along with these powerful gifts this position also brings emotional isolation in some form. In youth, they were usually socially isolated in some way, the ego undergoing difficult tests of the loss of love, death of loved ones, undue restriction, social ostracism, possibly even institutionalization, or a combination of these, at an early age, and often alone, without loving counsel. Rather than destroy the ego, this usually works to crystallize it, strengthen it, forcing it to feed on ideas, fantasies, on religious truths, or plans for the future, giving it great potential for the adult years of power.

These people seem complete unto themselves, cool, self-reliant, and secure within their own abilities, but they will always be vulnerable, deeply craving affection and commitment, and more or less terrified that they will never find it. In their own isolation, it is hard for them to see the need and vulnerability of others, and they may be capable of terrible coldness, and even cruelty, to those who need them. They may latch onto one person who they hope will give them all they crave in the way of emotional sustenance and commitment, but this can be neurotic in intensity and lead to an agonizing breakup. There may be a number of such relationships.

A woman with this position tends to choose a partner whose need is even greater than hers. Often, though, she will eventually come to resent her partner's dependency, not realizing that it was her own need to be needed that prompted her to form the relationship in the first place.

A man with this position will yearn for a partner who seems to be emotionally secure, often someone with more money or social position, one with a powerful or well-to-do father, or who is older and more successful in her career; or the well-kept mate or lover of a successful man, whom he will woo with all his power. These relationships usually have a hard time in reality. He may dedicate much time and effort to winning her (or him), then back out at the last minute out of fear of the emotional or financial demands of the relationship. Should the object of his dreams actually turn to him and begin to reveal an ordinary neediness of their own, he may even begin to hate them.

Death, imprisonment, and/or exile may mark the life; if not directly, possibly through someone else. In a group, they tend to stand apart in some way, isolated from the rest either by fate or by choice. In their isolation, they are vulnerable to the intrigues or enmity of groups and can be made into scapegoats or patsies, suffering condemnation, ostracism, or worse for doing the same things that others do with impunity.

The Sun in the Ninth House

These people are dreamers who are also doers. Courageous, pioneering, adventurous, and very demanding of themselves, they compare themselves with ideal models, heroes of history or fiction, rather than with ordinary people known to them. They tend to settle far from native roots. They are often very career-minded and will sacrifice home ties and stretch bonds of affection to the breaking point to achieve what they desire. Their search for meaning may cause them to change careers or, at least, to contemplate such a change. At any rate, they are always intent on achieving great things in some area (the location of the Sun's dispositor can give a clue to which area).

They are usually attractive, with a charisma that outshines any physical imperfection they may have and attracts others to them, a popularity they do not seek as they are intensely private, and protect their inner selves by becoming distant or polite at moments of potential intimacy. They are inclined to be truly intimate with very few. They may change their inner circle from time to time, but rarely seek to widen it.

Frequently exceedingly gifted in their field of interest, they seem to have a source of knowledge, inspiration, vision, insight that puts them above everyone else, causing legends to form around them. Often, they are creators of new ways of thinking, of new forms, higher standards, and newer, higher goals. Iconoclasts, they destroy the old ways of seeing and doing in order to find new ones. Willing to take risks for what they believe, they will sometimes risk everything (including their lives) in pursuit of impossible goals.

Although the ninth house is the political angle *par excellence,* for some reason the Sun here makes them somewhat politically vulnerable. They have strong political ideas and objectives, but tend to lack the finesse and diplomacy necessary for successful political maneuvering and the caution necessary for political survival. Therefore, although the Sun in the ninth gives them the necessary upward thrust to achieve high office, they will need trines to outer planets in the first or fifth houses, or planets in the tenth house, in order to remain in power.

The Sun in the Tenth House

This is one of the strongest testimonies of career success. Negative aspects in the chart must be extremely severe to counteract its effect. It gives a proud, calm, dignified bearing, with an air of authority and a charismatic quality that others admire and respect, though they are usually quiet and undemanding in attitude. They appear to rise to high position through little or no effort of their own, just by being in the right place at the right time.

At the same time, there is a loneliness here; events of early life operate in some way to set them apart from others so that their qualities of character and mind develop in solitude. They are gratified by the admiration they attract, but would gladly exchange it for the rollicking freedom of a close-knit group of life-long buddies with whom they can be totally at ease and let down their defenses—something they may imitate, or experience in passing, but rarely find for real, or for long.

Family relationships are extremely precious to them, and they may cling to their family ties and early-life relationships, sometimes to too great an extent (particularly women), thus blocking their own natural growth and development away from the family into broader and more effective spheres.

There is great power in this location of the Sun, but they are often unaware of it, or unwilling to use it, fearing the loneliness that comes with it. If they try and fail, it is always due to their lack of belief in themselves or their willingness to continue always to see themselves as the folks at home see them. They must learn to let go of the advice and opinions of others and make decisions on their own. Once they can do this, their rise will be rapid. The earlier they are on their own, the better, as the habit of making their own decisions and taking immediate action will carry them forward. They should steer clear of closely binding business partnerships at the outset, as these will often come to hamper them later. The warmth and trust they seek will come later from people who trust them and are supported by their strength and self-confidence: their employees, students, constituents, or their own children.

The Sun in the Eleventh House

This location of the Sun gives a strong and unshakable sense of self from early childhood on. They seem to know who they are and what they want from the beginning. Generally attractive, they can be intensely charismatic, in some cases projecting an almost godlike quality of higher knowledge, inner strength, or supernatural wisdom. Many kings, queens, emperors, heroes, and actors who portray heroes have the Sun here, as well as many great innovators, those who set new styles or start new ways of thinking and doing things. They go their own way and devil take the hindmost. They attract others to them, and they enjoy the company and the good times, but they also think nothing of pulling up stakes and setting forth on their own, leaving old friends behind forever. They feel confident in their ability to form new relationships when they need them.

They are charming and can project great warmth toward others, but are not at all sentimental and rarely create needs out of habit. Those who are close to them may come to be very angry at them for this cold streak. They are exceedingly class conscious and, though they may appear to be completely democratic in their treatment of others, in truth they will usually jettison one set of friends for another group higher on the social ladder, one that is closer to the glory land of big names, easy living, and classy surroundings.

They are capable of working along their own lines for years without compromising their integrity, either believing that their way will win out in the end or not really giving a damn, more interested in doing it their own way than in any eventual success. However, if and when success does come, it usually comes as much from their being adept at social manipulation as from the quality of their efforts.

The Sun in the Twelfth House

Here the ego is under great pressure. They have the same powerful ego thrust as those with the Sun rising, but are met by so much opposition in youth that the ego either swells to immense proportions to crush out all opposition, or it retreats from battle altogether. In youth, they are so determinedly and uncompromisingly themselves that they attract the opposition of family members, schoolmates, friends, and neighbors, who never cease to give them a hard time.

They will learn to live with others the hard way. Some truly learn to compromise, and some to dissemble and intrigue, pretending to compromise while pulling strings and making secret deals to get what they want, while some retreat from all confrontation, if they can. Those who attempt to retreat often find that life has a way of coming after them and forcing confrontations that they would rather avoid. Some become monsters of egotism, seeing enemies everywhere and crushing all who stand in their path. Anyone not with them will be considered against them, and even friends may be suspected of being enemies in disguise. Still others will go the opposite way and come to suspect their own egos, and ego itself, as a negative, selfish force. These people will be inclined to champion the voiceless underdogs of the world and give endlessly of themselves to others.

Most people with this position have an intensely private side that they keep hidden from all but their most intimate friends. On the other hand, there are those who go to the opposite extreme and live only for the spotlight and, as their close associates know, have absolutely no private life at all.

They have an instinct for the public mind and can capitalize on (or even create) popular trends, though there is always a strong streak of the purely individual in everything they do that brands it theirs.

They are usually quiet on the surface and become talkative only with those closest to them, though even this can go to the opposite extreme, in which case they can be compulsive talkers, pouring out a continual stream of egotistical self-applause.

They are usually involved with an institution for awhile, either as a patient in a hospital, a student in a reform school or orphanage, an inmate of a prison, or as a worker in one of these facilities.

Given to working for causes, they can even create a cause in order to give themselves something to work for.

The overall truism about the twelfth-house Sun is that it tends to go to extremes; what sort of extremes will be indicated by the aspects to the Sun and its dispositor. Often, these people will go to one extreme in youth, then overcompensate at mid-life by swinging to the opposite extreme, coming finally late in life to more perspective and a more comfortable position near the middle of the road.

Those who rise to power have a tendency to misuse it. The tendency to go to extremes and to vacillate from one extreme to another can have terrible consequences, both for them and for their constituents. Those who become successful in other fields often carry a reputation for misbehavior or suffering; for instance, actors or writers may prefer to portray martyrs, villains, or underdogs, than more upbeat types. In almost any field they may have a reputation for being hard to get along with.

Mars Through the Houses

Mars, like the Roman god for which it is named, has always been representative of the Warrior. It symbolizes the powerful masculine principle in nature that boldly takes charge of events, seeks to dominate everything it encounters, and yet is ever seeking its opposite, the magnetic, mysterious, hidden, beautiful feminine, symbolized by Venus. These happen to be the two planets that flank the Earth: Venus to the inside, closer to the Sun, the center of authority and of life, and Mars to the outside, away from the Sun, toward the rest of the Universe and the outer rim of the solar system. They form a pair; their union in organic life is the sexual nature, the means of reproducing, and their relationship in a chart speaks of the love nature of the individual, their sexual nature, their ability and drive to reproduce successfully, both in a physical sense (to have children) and in an emotional sense (to express the self in deeds and works).

The Earth circles the Sun and the Moon circles the Earth. Mercury and Venus circle the Sun on orbits that lie *inside* Earth's orbit; so these are known as *interior* planets, all intimately part of the Earth/Sun relationship. Mars is the first planet to lie outside the Earth/Sun system, the first of the *exterior* planets. Mars is the closest planet to Earth to form oppositions to the Sun, which may be part of the reason for the energy attributed to Mars.*

During the time that such an opposition lasts, the Earth is subjected to a pull from the Sun on one side and an opposite pull from Mars on the other. So that where Mercury and Venus, whose abilities work best in harmony with others, are weakened by oppositions, Mars is strengthened, a valiant courage for opposing what is intolerable being part of its nature. When Mars appears to be moving more rapidly than the Earth and "passes" it after an opposition, it gives a push to Earth's magnetic field, and consequently a push to the developments of events on Earth, particularly those related to the matters ruled by the sign it occupies at the time. When it appears to be going slower than Earth, and Earth "passes" it, it is considered to be in retrograde motion, which manifests a dragging quality on the

---

* The Moon forms oppositions to the Sun, of course: we call that *Full Moon*, but the Moon orbits the Earth, which makes its dynamic different from the other planets.

energy it exchanges with Earth at that time. Of course, planets never actually slow to a halt and reverse motion, they only appear to. A good metaphor for the two situations would be the sensation of being passed on the highway by a big truck; the wash of air, the sensation of being pulled forward in its wake, as opposed to the sensation of passing a slower truck, which appears to be slowing down and even moving backward.

It is desirable to have many aspects to Mars as it shows a complex where energy is put to many uses.

No aspects to Mars is very difficult; they have a tough time getting things started and keeping them going. One or two hard aspects with no relief builds tremendous tension that may burst forth into destructive acts. Nor is all harmonious aspects a good thing, as it lulls Mars into a kind of flywheel spin that goes nowhere.

At least one square or opposition adds power to a chart, although too many hard aspects with no relief will make life an endless series of confrontations, and build tremendous tensions that may burst forth in destructive acts.

A weak Mars makes it hard for a person to take a strong stand against negative persons or conditions. The worst situation for Mars is to have no aspects. Then it is like having an engine with the fan belt disconnected. Such individuals have a tough time getting things started and keeping them going.

Mars on the angles gives tremendous energy. How this will be used, and whether for good or ill, will be shown by the sign location, dispositor, etc.

The location of Mars in a chart will show where there is a focus of animal energy available for the matters of that house, and the sign that it is in will determine what quality the energy possesses. Mars is most intense and straightforward in fire signs; strongest in Aries and most steadfast in Leo and, although fluctuating in Sagittarius, capable of great bursts of effort. It is also good in the earth signs where it is slowed but gains in stamina, except in Taurus, where the rooted and Venusian qualities of the sign can slow it down too much. Mars is variable in air signs, where aspects affect it strongly, but where it always has much energy for talking, writing, teaching, and so on. It is uncomfortable in water signs, where its fiery nature is bogged down. In water, it is forced to operate on the emotional plane to too great an extent, and not enough on the physical, which is where it is most comfortable. Although it is possible to accomplish much with Mars in water—the combination of fire and water make steam, and steam can drive mighty engines—it is emotionally difficult. Mars is by nature strong-willed, not self-willed. It longs to share its strength and glory, whereas water turns it in on itself, and therefore makes Mars too concerned with self. Of course, having its dispositor in a fire sign helps a good deal (such as Mars in Cancer, Moon in Leo).

In a life span, Mars rules the years roughly between thirty-five to fifty, when early training ripens into leadership, when we realize that it's now or never for achieving our goals, and when we begin to take control, not only of our own lives, but often of others' lives as well. These are the years of power.

Mars in the First House

Mars rising gives tremendous vitality, drive and will. It is impossible to keep anyone with this placement down. If one thing doesn't work, they'll figure out something else. If other factors testify to a career, this will give impetus, competitive spirit, and follow-through. These people will go crazy from boredom if they haven't got something to keep them busy at all times.

Women with Mars rising can have a somewhat hard or unprepossessing appearance if there is no aspect from the Moon, Venus, or Jupiter to soften it. If there is, Mars adds fire and intensity, and gives a compelling force to their appearance that commands attention. Women with Mars rising have a tough row to hoe, but if they are honest with themselves they know that they wouldn't have it any other way.

Mars in this location adds great physicality to the nature. It adds fight to the nature, the will to never say die. Unless its fire is greatly diminished by sign or aspect, there will probably be at least one knock-down-drag-out physical fight at some time, usually in youth. It's an especially good position for soldiers, athletes, and dancers, but it also is good for any career as it gives great stamina, staying power, and courage.

These people seek thrills and challenges. They may either die young from taking risks, or live long and hearty lives. There is great gusto here, a lust for life. They are extremely competitive and need regular physical competition so their competitive nature won't cause problems within their friendships and love relationships.

They are not inclined to be deep thinkers unless other aspects show it. Even if there are thought aspects, these people will rely mainly on instinct and inspiration. Action is a passion with them. They love to be in motion.

They have big appetites and can be lustful, willful, and gluttonous, unless other aspects hold them back. They tend to get into positions of authority through their energetic efforts, and also because they don't like taking orders themselves. If they do acquire authority, they tend to be somewhat insensitive toward those beneath them and to use power to satisfy personal desires. Many kings and emperors have Mars rising or conjunct the Sun; not only those who win their own glory, but also those who inherit it and go on to use it effectively.

With good aspects they become like smooth-running machines in middle life, once past their early lustful rebellious years. By middle life, they tend to become serious, dedicated, and able to command respect.

They are inclined to be accident-prone, depending on the aspects to Mars, and must watch out that they don't go too fast and lose control. They often have a scar on the face or head, or on that part of the body ruled by the sign Mars is in. Unless aspects are really bad, they lose their tendency towards accidents in middle life. With good aspects, they are agile and deft with their hands, bodies, and minds from youth until death. If there are oppositions or inconjuncts to Mars, and no trine or sextile to relieve them, there will be great stress, an unresolved physical tension, a rigidity, an inability to move or act, that may end in illness or accident.

They are usually slender in youth from activity. If Mars is in a water or earth sign, they may gain weight in later years from overindulgence in food and drink, though some stay trim throughout life due to self control.

If Mars is square Mercury, they are witty, but may overwork themselves. A rising Mars square the Sun tends to overwork to the point where there may be a breakdown.

Mars in the Second House

These people don't want to deny themselves any sexual experience if Mars is in fire or water. They are more likely to accept restraint in air or earth. This makes for a hectic emotional life. Out of forty-seven celebrity charts with this Mars, only four were those of women (and one of them took a man's name). Women with this Mars usually have too exciting or time-consuming an emotional life to have anything to spare for a career.

In other ways it can be a conservative position, reinforcing basic values: home, family, mother, mate, church, and so on, although the drive for sex experience can act as an undertow. If there isn't frequent sex, there is the desire for it; or, in air, a great deal of thought about it. These people usually have an aura of sexual power, machismo, or seductive femininity. With other factors that indicate the same thing it can testify to homosexuality, or at least to some homosexual or bisexual experiences. With very severe bad aspects, there can be serious sex deviations and problems.

There is a lot of drive and energy in this location but, unless there are strong humanitarian testimonies, it will be primarily motivated by a desire for self-gratification. They are usually well aware of what side their bread is buttered on, and will rarely act so as to endanger income, property, or social status. If social determinants prevent them from gratifying their sexual desires it will set up a terrific conflict within them and they will try hard to find a way to have it both ways.

They are apt to be rather cynical and not terribly idealistic, unless other aspects show that strongly. They are also apt to be loners, and to stand apart from the rest of society in some way. They may feel somewhat misunderstood or isolated. With bad aspects, this can become paranoia, wife-beating, bar-brawling, or such; even (with other testimony) the total isolation of madness.

There is the danger of an early removal from the action; exile, loss of power in a coup, or something of the sort that keeps them on the sidelines for a long period. This position of Mars requires good supportive aspects and the utmost patience to bring anything to fruition.

Mars in the Third House

Those with a third house Mars are fearless about exploring anything that is new and untried. Eternally youthful, they are forever in search of new and better methods, better places and ways to live, deeper and more fundamental truths. It is a good location for inventors and scientists, although anyone with this Mars will be inventive and have the true scientific spirit. There is an experimental attitude towards life; if one thing does not work out, they'll try another. Once something has been tried, though, they tend to lose interest, so unless Mars is in Capricorn or Virgo, this isn't a particularly good aspect for business or career, unless other factors show it, such as Mars in Capricorn or Virgo. Unless they have the Sun, Moon, Venus, Neptune, or Jupiter in a water sign, they will be likely to experiment with their emotional life as well.

Their energy level fluctuates at this angle; they must learn how to work hard and then relax completely, or they will slow to a crawl. They need to keep several projects going that require different energy levels so that when one kind of energy is used up they can switch to another.

They are good communicators, able to convey and understand ideas without confusion; unless there is much contact with Neptune or the Moon, in which case they learn by doing and may have a hard time expressing themselves verbally. They are inclined to speak too rapidly and sometimes too forcefully. If there are bad aspects from Uranus and/or Mercury, they may suffer from a speech impediment of some sort.

This is an excellent position for athletes such as swimmers, tennis players, golfers, or equestrians, where the accent is more on form and style and less on sheer power. It is excellent for entertainers of all kinds, especially dancers. It contributes to the ability to blend several talents, such as dancing, singing, comedy, mime, and acting, or writing, performing, directing, and producing. Whatever they choose to do, they are usually graceful at all the social arts, able to speak well and amusingly, able to do the latest dances and to dress stylishly.

They are quick to learn in school, though they may get in trouble for being too restless or too outspoken in class. They don't like to sit still for too long, and always need plenty of exercise or they will be nervous and jumpy, or will rely on substances like coffee, cigarettes, pills, etc., to keep them going. Jogging, walking, and riding bicycles are much healthier ways for them to use, stimulate, and regulate their energies.

They are apt to have a highly competitive relationship with at least one sibling and, at least once in their lives, a physical or verbal battle with a neighbor. If there are squares to Mars there may be many such battles.

They love to be on the move and will drop everything and take off at a moment's notice. They are good drivers, though they tend to go too fast and, with squares or oppositions, may be accident-prone. They love to drive anything from a tractor to an airplane and make excellent race drivers and pilots. They love to explore, take dares, set records, and do things no one has ever done before.

Mars in the Fourth House

This is a difficult spot for Mars; square to the Ascendant, opposed to the Midheaven, and submerged in the lowest sector of the chart. However, these very difficulties often stimulate it to great effort, so that although it doesn't always show forth as great external accomplishment, it almost always shows a life of great growth and inner development.

This placement almost always indicates a heavy relationship with the mother that marks the entire life. The mother is apt to be domineering, though if aspects are supportive, this may simply show as strength and support without her will being imposed to too great a degree. In any case, the mother outshines the father, who may die or leave the home during childhood or youth. If the Moon is here, or Neptune, or if Mars is in Cancer or Pisces, there is sorrow added—the mother suffers, is ill, unhappy, or hysterical. Or she may die, leaving them with lifelong emotional pain and guilt. This can result in alcoholism and, possibly (with enough other testimony), suicide.

In a man's chart, Mars in the fourth is apt to make him strong-willed, sometimes even harsh or cruel toward his wife and children, perhaps to compensate for having to endure his mother's problems. Having children of his own may appear to him to be a burden and a sorrow rather than a joy. In a woman's chart, it makes it hard for her to be receptive toward other women, particularly older women, and she may be unresponsive to her own children, due to pent-up anger or grief.

A fourth-house Mars with squares, inconjuncts, and oppositions almost always points to a hectic, disorderly home in childhood, with the possibility of physical or emotional violence. This difficult home atmosphere may be reproduced in the adult home as well. People with these chart conditions would benefit from therapy.

This may not be the easiest location for Mars, but it can act as a goad, prodding them toward self-mastery and accomplishment, if only to escape or rise above the early home environment. It forces them to consider basic values, to decide what is real versus what isn't, to set priorities, and to act upon them. It is the sign of those who must pull themselves up by their bootstraps. It is a sort of "make or break" factor; they will either succumb and allow life to turn them into something they themselves cannot respect, or they will fight to improve themselves and their lot. In the one case, they will be self-pitying, filled with anger and blame and inclined to take out their feelings on those weaker; in the other, they will be philosophical, feel pity for those who mistreated or neglected them, and be kind and tender to those weaker than themselves.

It gives a good deal of strength to withstand the ups and downs of fortune in either case, and generally gives a firm grip on life. It can testify to a long, productive life, or to an early, usually violent death, depending on various other factors. It can also be partial testimony to death by accident. In any case, there will probably be a close call early in life that shocks them into caution and awareness.

Mars at this angle doesn't have the power that it has on the other angles to bring things about rapidly, but it does have stick-to-it-iveness, follow-through and bounce-back, and it can accomplish a lot over a life-time. It does give the power to start something new, a new way of doing things, new ideas, that take a lifetime of dedication to instill, and often bring more renown to those who come after than to those whose vision it was in the first place. Sometimes it means that they have a greater effect on later generations than on their own.

Often, it means that they leave home and live the rest of their lives far from native roots. If Mars is in Gemini or Sagittarius, they may never stay anywhere long enough to put down roots of their own. If it is in earth or water signs, they may build their own home, or sacrifice much to acquire land and property or a home of their own. With bad aspects, there is danger to the home, particularly from fire. It is a good location for construction workers, builders, and architects.

Mars in the Fifth House

This location of Mars gives a powerful will. It is a partial testimony to the self-made man or woman. It is a very strong testimony to career success. Mars at the 120-degree (trine) angle to both the Ascendant and the Midheaven gives a powerful drive that can be applied to any chosen end.

These people exert a magnetic fascination for others but as performers they have a hard time because they find it so difficult to take direction, except from those few they truly respect. They may have a hard time in childhood because they hate to be told what to do. They were eager to grow up and form their lives for themselves. They can't work for others for long, but must control their own destiny, and will, as soon as possible. Sometimes, they launch out into business for themselves at an astonishingly early age.

They are very sexual, and, if there is other testimony to homosexuality, this will strengthen it. Bisexuality is possible with both sexes. The sex drive is intense and, with oppositions and squares and no trines or sextiles, it can be a problem, as ungratified desire can lead to violence of some sort. They are passionate and generous in love and seek to gratify their partner as well as themselves. They are often too rapid in their responses for others, and must learn to go slowly. Their intense competitiveness can harm love relationships until they learn to use it in appropriate ways.

They are inclined to have children—possibly lots of them, with more males than females, all rambunctious and hard to control, but healthy, strong, and eager to learn. With bad aspects, there may be danger to the life of a child through fire, fever, or accident.

They are very creative and generally have several hobbies that have a way of turning into income-producers. They usually like knives and metal tools and will try to become proficient in their use. They may also like guns, even though they may not totally approve of their use, appreciating them for their workmanship, power, etc., rather than their killing potential. They enjoy using their bodies and find it easy to stay in shape through regular exercise. This is an excellent position for a professional athlete or dancer. They are highly competitive and enjoy sports and games where their competitiveness and combativeness can find a safe and enjoyable outlet.

They are gamblers and are usually lucky. They like horse racing, card games, and all forms of wagering. They like taking risks of all sorts. If forced to stick too close to the straight and narrow, they get bored and become bad company, irritable and prone to temper.

Parents of children with a fifth-house Mars must learn to let them discover their own limits earlier than most children do, because an overreaction against authority can bring on accidents or illness. They require training, but the child should set the pace, the parent acting only as watchdog. They rebel if forced but, if given their own lead, will forge ahead with confidence.

People with Mars in the fifth are excellent natural leaders and will pull others with them wherever they go. Their charisma is usually nonverbal; they will have an intimate circle who know them while few outsiders will have any knowledge of what they are really like. Sometimes that circle is very small, but they don't care. It can be an aspect of narcissism, too much self-interest, yet they continue to attract others who do not know them and who never will.

Although they love freedom, they also know that nothing happens without discipline. They are usually orderly at bottom, even if the surface sometimes looks a little confused, and demand that subordinates be the same. They are good teachers, inspiring but demanding. They do their best as leader of a team, a small, flexible unit that reports to a respected superior (if to anyone) but functions apart. They don't like bosses looking over their shoulder, and they don't enjoy managing large groups. If they can they will turn such a job over to someone else. It is a good position for an independent worker, someone who generates their own business or ideas.

With Mars in water, they are extremely passionate, may be unreasonable or moody at times, may fantasize a lot, and may be in danger of going off the deep end over love or artistic projects. They may also be inclined to drink too much. With Mars in air, they are usually very thoughtful of co-workers, lovers, friends, students, and are forceful and independent thinkers. With Mars in fire, they may be too quick and too hot, self-willed and over-competitive, at least in youth. In earth, they will be quite self-controlled and more likely to work steadily at a lifelong career than if Mars is in one of the other elements.

If Mars is in a cardinal sign, these individuals have strong, irresistible, but flexible wills. If it is in a fixed sign, they will be strong-willed, but inclined to be stubborn and inflexible. In a mutable sign, their own self-development may be more important to them than maintaining a career thrust.

Mars in the Sixth House

This is an aspect of obedience. Mars in the sixth house gives the ability to work diligently, but they must find a field they like or they'll suffer from psychosomatic ills, accidents in the workplace, or fights with co-workers. Mars here is more or less trine the Midheaven but inconjunct the Ascendant, so the energy moves more easily from the ninth and tenth houses, the houses of bosses and "superiors," than it does from the first, that of the self; with the result that this is inclined to be somewhat of a self-sacrificing position. These people will often work themselves into the ground for the good of the company. With tenth-house planets, this is a good placement for a team athlete or coach, a member of a ballet corps, or a ballet teacher. Most men with this Mars location spend some time in military service. Some make it a career.

These people are slow and hard to train as children but, once trained, they become good, dependable workers at whatever they do. This Mars is good in any field where daily practice is necessary. They may take a long time learning to practice, but once the habit is developed they will adhere to it religiously from then on.

As children, they are the opposite of those with Mars in the fifth; they must be pushed. They need early training and discipline, as the older they get, the more ingrained bad habits will become. They may seek to avoid work if Mars is in Leo, Sagittarius, Libra, or Pisces, or if it is conjunct or opposite Saturn, the Moon, or Neptune. There can be trouble with relatives and bosses over lack of work effort until they find their true field. Those with Mars in Aries, Cancer, Virgo, Scorpio, or Capricorn can work hard at anything, if they must.

A sixth-house Mars needs a square or other hard aspect to give it a kick from time to time, or they may fall into a rut, working for too long at the same job and living a life that leads nowhere. One way out is to develop a hobby by constant practice. Eventually, this will lead to a freer and more satisfying existence.

Mars in the Seventh House

This Mars gives a combative nature; they won't take anything lying down. Argumentative, it seems as though no matter whatever it is, they're against it. They have trouble getting along with people, so those with Sun or Mars in fire or earth signs will get a reputation for being touchy and hard to deal with, while those with Sun or Mars in air or water will mask their irritation in order to avoid confrontation. They are compelled by their strong sex drive to find a partner, but have a hard time staying with anyone. Part of the reason for this is that they tend to choose other combative types, so the fur will fly from time to time (or all the time). At least one relationship will end in anger and total misunderstanding. It takes them years to learn how to live with others.

First, they must learn to live with themselves. Often mistreated in some way, neglected or ignored by one or both parents in childhood, they take out their anger on everyone else until they begin to see what they are doing and learn to release the energy in other, less destructive ways. With Mars in Cancer or Pisces, the combativeness is modified. It may show as passive/aggressive behavior, or it may be turned inward, leading to illness. These people should always involve themselves in competitive sports so as to absorb their combative energies and keep other areas free from it.

If the Moon is on an angle, this Mars can be dangerous; violence may be done to them or by them. Yet if they can learn to harness their energies, and to live with themselves and others, much can be achieved with the seventh-house Mars, as the energy, properly applied, is endless.

These people are often lonely and feel misunderstood by others. Something has hardened them to the outside world, diminishing their natural sensitivity to others. They feel misunderstood, but it is really they who misunderstand others and misinterpret their motives. It is hard for others to break through this tough shell. In fact, it is impossible, until they are willing to come out from behind their defenses.

They will often have a relationship with an athlete, someone athletic in nature, or who enjoys sports as a pastime, possibly someone in the police or the military. With bad aspects to Mars, they may have a relationship with someone violent, or someone who has suffered from violence, or who has a dangerous occupation or lifestyle.

They are tough opponents and do well in anything where fight is required. Although oppositions or conjunctions to the Moon or Saturn may make them fearful, once the fat is in the fire, watch out!

Good aspects, particularly trines to planets in the eleventh house, will modify the difficulties of this position, giving them the power to control themselves and diminishing the touchiness. However, the basic stress of opposition from the Ascendant and square from the Midheaven to this most energetic and forceful of planets is hard to modify.

Mars in the Eighth House

Still waters run deep—and strong. These people have a charisma that attracts others to them, but they are reserved and hard to know. There is a restlessness of the soul that will lead them far from native soil and values on at least one far-flung excursion. Many venture so far from home that there is no return. They march to a different drummer than their community of origin. Their drive is towards different goals than those of family and early friends. Often misunderstood in youth, they seek a distant ideal that rarely or never materializes and, even if it does, often only briefly.

They are inclined to sacrifice too much in relationships at least once, which may cause them to become fearful of the emotional demands of relationships. Escape from a relationship can be the motivating force behind big changes in their lives, moving far from home, taking a job in a foreign country.

They are highly sexual, which brings problems. They may repress their sexuality, resulting in psychological problems of various kinds. With Mars in a fixed sign, there may be homosexual desires; other aspects will show if these will be expressed, or denied and repressed. Frequently, in air or mutable signs, homosexual experiences are brief and occur in youth as part of sexual development. Their sexual development is so important to them that it may rule their lives.

Even their death is often related to sex in some way, with links to the loss, failure, or frustration of a sexual relationship. They will often have a close brush with death at some point in their lives. Mars in the eighth is partial testimony to a sudden death.

Mars in the Ninth and Tenth Houses

Mars at the top of the chart gives a powerful thrust toward recognition. Whether this is for good or ill will be shown by Jupiter, Saturn, and the aspects to Mars and its dispositor. If these are mostly supportive, there will be early and enduring success. Stimulating aspects from the Sun, Uranus, or the Moon, without balancing trines, bring recklessness, notoriety, an early rise followed by downfall, and/or early death. Oppositions, conjunctions, or squares from Neptune or Saturn can slow or deny recognition, causing intense frustration. Mars conjunct Neptune can distort recognition, causing them to be misunderstood and their deeds misinterpreted (down through history, if they are famous, or infamous).

This Mars gives great energy and drive. They will never say die. They are extremely combative and competitive and, though they frequently mask it with charm, they have wills of iron, unyielding and enduring, particularly with Mars in fire or earth. They are inclined to make enemies by their methods, but they usually delight in enemies, using them to strengthen their combative or competitive techniques.

Mars is more self-questioning in the ninth house, more political and less autocratic in technique, more open, more inclined to give up and let go under stress. It is stronger in the tenth house, more enduring. In either house, there is an inclination to displays of bad temper, or, if there are very tense aspects to Mars, fits, hysterical tantrums, or some kind of periodic outburst of pent-up energy. Extremely physical, they need sports or some other kind of stabilizing physical outlet for their energies.

As leaders, they are inclined to be harsh or even cruel to their followers, driving them too hard; though, if this tendency is held in check, they are a vitalizing force for those around them, a source of energy and motivation. They are inclined to drive themselves mercilessly and may be rather humorless, at least about themselves and their needs, rights, and immediate goals. They see their own rights very clearly, but not always so clearly the rights of others.

This is definitely one of the signatures of a career chart. In a woman's chart she will have a career come hell or high water, even if she is married, has ten kids, and lives in the Outback. With Mars in the ninth, she may subordinate her own desires and work for her husband's success, but inside she will resent it. With Mars in the tenth, she will get busy and find a way to do it herself.

This highly-placed Mars makes people restless, not content to stay put for long. They will probably travel far from home and experience much. Success does not usually come in their place of birth or, if so, only after traveling and experiencing other places. They have a hard time getting along with other strong-minded people, including authority figures, and moves are often initiated after altercations with other members of the family or community.

As children, they must be driven hard physically to develop their endurance and use up their energies so they won't erupt in temper or get into trouble. Pile on the chores: they'll rise to the challenge and, even if they grumble, down deep they'll be grateful. They should be given the freedom to roam and to discover their own limits, but should be held strictly to account for wrongdoing and punished fairly. Grounding is a nonviolent and effective punishment for these restless souls. This elevated Mars provides a momentum that is hard to overcome and should be trained, while it is still young and pliable, to live by the rules as much as is possible.

Mars in the Eleventh House

With an eleventh house Mars there is a strong determination to move continuously toward permanent goals that are fixed in youth and rarely questioned later. If there are other planets in the eleventh house, the goals may be mixed or, where the planets are not congenial, there may be confusion or conflict between two or more goals. However, no matter what the difficulties, these individuals will struggle on toward their goals in spite of everything.

They have a great deal of energy for getting what they want, are not easily talked out of going for it, and will keep it once they've got it. If not actually "born to the purple," they are inclined to be social climbers and like hanging out with the Four Hundred, shining by their reflected light.

These people have strong personalities and have a hard time yielding to the desires of others. Often, they will fight to have their way about something that they don't care about anymore, just on principle. They may suffer inner stress over the conflict between doing things the way they want and doing them the way they must if they are to "get ahead."

This Mars gives great power to act on ideas. It is good for an artist, writer, or any kind of independent creator. In the realm of ideas, it is possible for them to work well with groups, but they will usually do best on their own.

With Mars in fixed signs, they are unbelievably stubborn. They must be in charge and are not particularly sensitive to those they are bossing. In cardinal signs, there will be more perspective; they will be excellent at setting and achieving goals. In mutable signs, they will be more flexible, better with coworkers and groups. They will be more able to upgrade goals in later life, with spiritual goals more likely.

Often, women with this location of Mars are attracted to men of the same nature, and they will form a team to achieve common goals; although sometimes an overly-competitive attitude makes teamwork difficult, even impossible. Women with this Mars should not marry early, as often they will come to regret it later. Neither sex should marry until they know themselves well enough to tolerate someone else over a long period of time.

Mars in the Twelfth House

Mars is very strong at this angle; those with this position are capable of intense effort. They will have an early experience that teaches them restraint (if it doesn't do them in), although it may take many lessons before they learn to hold back when necessary. They are capable of miraculous feats of effort and will. Types of effort will range from the spiritual—lives dedicated to high spiritual goals—to the lowest levels of self-gratification, but the power is present to do what they will.

The Mars energy is so primal and strong at this angle that it is hard for these people to be rational and objective about their inner drives and cravings. In youth, they may be troublesome to those near and dear because of the scrapes they get into. They are capable of rising high in life and achieving much, but are always susceptible to having their cart overturned, usually due to their own recklessness (physical in earth and fire, verbal in air, emotional in water).

If Mars is close to the Ascendant there is more persistence; more power to hold on, to learn from adversity and go on to win, and to try over and over in spite of difficulties. Mars in the middle of the twelfth house inclines toward giving in to defeat, or to a loss of control so great that the recuperative powers have no chance to act.

If aspects to Mars are not good, there may be trouble with the law, time spent in jail, or serious accidents and time spent in hospitals.

4

Jupiter Through the Houses

Jupiter has always been known as the "greater benefic" (Venus being the "lesser benefic") and, as such, its placement in a chart brings strong positive energy to the matters of the house where it is located. Jupiter and Saturn are the outermost planets of the solar system as it was known before the discoveries of the "modern planets," discoveries that required the development of lenses, telescopes, and other modern technologies. Jupiter is far and away the biggest planet in the solar system, and shines very slightly by its own light. It also supports a large number of satellites, or little planets, of its own. Perhaps for these reasons, the Theosophists believe that Jupiter is evolving into a star, or another

Sun. It takes Jupiter twelve years to orbit the entire zodiac, spending about a year in each sign.

Jupiter was the king of the gods in the ancient pagan religions, with Saturn his father (and Uranus his grandfather), so that Jupiter and Saturn taken together represent what one might call "the God principle": Jupiter the gift-giving and forgiving aspect of God, while Saturn represents the disciplinarian—stern, demanding, ready to punish transgression. Jupiter gives and Saturn takes, and both, by their actions on us, cause us to grow as individuals.

Jupiter has many of the same qualities as the Sun, but without the egoism. Where the Sun represents the father, Jupiter represents uncles and patrons, less controlling, harsh, and demanding, but also perhaps less directly involved, less concerned.

There is a remote quality to Jupiter. It gives, but gives the way a lord gives gifts to his peasants at holiday time, somewhat automatically. There is an odd thing about Jupiter, in that often it denies at first that which it gives in abundance later in life. In general, it gives mostly to the second half of life, while Venus gives more to the first half.

Jupiter relates specifically to material benefits only in the more material signs and houses, but it always relates to gifts of the soul: wisdom, understanding, tolerance, inspiration, gifts than can conflict with ordinary, mundane goals, at least in the beginning. It represents hope, which is ultimately the fruit of age, the experienced knowledge that every cloud has a silver lining, that what goes down must come back up sooner or later. Thus, people with Jupiter on the angles always seem optimistic and cheerful, at least to outsiders, although their lives may be no less difficult than anyone else's.

Jupiter relates particularly to the so-called "golden years" (vaguely between forty-five or fifty and sixty-five to seventy), the harvest years when we reap what we have sown in youth and benefit from the work and plans of a lifetime. This is also the time when our wisdom guides the whole of society; most important social and political decisions are made by persons in their fifties, sixties, and seventies.

Jupiter on the angles increases both pride and luck, and gives good looks, charm, and charisma. In the body, it is related to vision and the brain, is said to rule the liver, and has something to do with the sense of taste. It rules the principles of expansion, multiplication, of exponential increase.

Jupiter in the First House

People with Jupiter rising always have the courage of their convictions, and often great physical courage as well. Often they are engaged in a lifelong pursuit of truth through systems and ideas. They are natural philosophers, seekers of wisdom. Because they love the truth and seek it, for themselves, they scorn lies and will rarely tell a genuine lie, though they will often stretch the mundane truth so much in the telling that a less-imaginative eyewitness has a hard time recognizing it. They are boiling over with creative imagination and must have some area in which to use it or they will drive their loved ones crazy. This is an ideal position for a salesman, politician, or minister. It is also excellent for a writer, artist, or performer.

Generally good to look at, with an appearance handsome, noble, or dignified rather than "cute," Jupiter gives them a charisma that outshines any physical imperfection. They have an innate sense of style and generally dress to perfection, except in cases where the truthseeker scorns the material level to too great an extent, causing them to scorn mere appearance; or to the opposite extreme, where Jupiter becomes overblown by aspects of the Moon, Sun, Neptune, or Venus, causing them to overdress, overeat, and overdo in all areas of self-gratification. Their delight in "dressing up" extends into adulthood, and they love to get in costume for plays, masquerades, parties, and so forth.

They are always charming, good storytellers, and, in most cases, good listeners as well. They are born diplomats, courteous, at ease with all kinds of people, the life of any party. They are usually witty and entertaining speakers, but so generous in spirit that, unless other aspects harden the ego, they will rarely keep the center of the stage for longer than is their fair share.

They are proud, sometimes to a fault—usually too proud to stoop to low behavior of any kind, although the definition of what constitutes low behavior will vary from one individual to another. Their only real faults are their lack of humility and a tendency to go to extremes. They believe in themselves and the rightness of what they do, and are not inclined to question themselves. If they achieve power, they are generally noble in exercising it, unless aspects in the chart show a tendency to go to extremes in self indulgence. In that case, the added power can make them grotesque in their hedonism.

Jupiter rising is often the sign of one who does it all by himself or herself ("Operation Bootstraps"), not because there is no one to help, but because they are too proud to ask. They sometimes get furthest by working for a cause, as they are perfectly capable of asking when it is for someone else.

If Jupiter is isolated—not related to other planets by aspect—they will tend to isolate themselves from the rest of the world, setting themselves up as higher somehow, wiser, more honorable, more worthy in some way, not condescending to associate with the lesser folk around them; kind and responsive to those who seek them out, but disdaining to seek out others themselves.

Jupiter rising can be the sign of one whose father failed to give them enough love, wisdom, or financial security, so that they are forced to seek it elsewhere and secure it for themselves. The lifetime search for truth can also be a lifetime search for a father figure, a guru, a patron—one who knows and cares.

Jupiter in the Second House

Once Jupiter gets over the cusp of the second house, it ceases to indicate those who get along on their own and becomes the sign of those who depend on patrons or the good will of others, so that locating the cusp accurately can be important.

Jupiter at this angle is concerned about religious and philosophical ideas, but does not let them get in the way of obtaining the bread and butter. This is an excellent position for an artist or performer as it guarantees patronage and support. It is a good sign for doing what one wants in life; although, unless Jupiter is trine the Midheaven, it is not so good for a career as it relaxes the anxious, upward thrust for sheer survival that is usually necessary for successful career efforts. At times of stress, rather than forge a new path in solitude, this one often turns to home, family, or old friends for strokes and needed support. Young people with this position may find it hard to leave the comfort of the family nest.

If Jupiter is trine the Midheaven, it assures a smooth and easy path to success, frequently with little conscious effort. They just seem to get all the breaks, are in the right place at the right time, and succeed more through good luck than through hard work. The further Jupiter is from a trine to the Midheaven (or a planet in the ninth or tenth), the more work is needed.

Good things come easily to these people, but it takes other aspects to ensure that they stay. They tend to be big spenders who don't devote enough time and thought to practical matters. They tend to be "easy come, easy go."

Jupiter in the Third House

At this angle, Jupiter gives a golden gift of communication skills, the ability to inspire others and to win them over. These people are frequently good singers or musicians. This is a good placement also for an actor, politician, minister, psychologist, salesman, or teacher. It is good for writers, though they may find it hard to settle down to work.

A third house Jupiter is inclined to variety in the love life. They like to play the field.

They enjoy school and school days and school friends, but find it difficult to concentrate hard enough to do well in school. The mind is easily distracted into philosophical backwaters, into ideas, dreams, ideals, and away from the cold pursuit of facts, figures, grade averages, etc., that lead to goals and diplomas. The mind is expansive, concerned with overall truths, not with detail. They do well in communications fields but often need others to do their fact-finding for them.

An older brother or sister is often important in helping them find their niche in life and, wherever they are, they will find kind, helpful, and frequently well-to-do and high-placed neighbors and acquaintances who will give support.

Jupiter in the Fourth House

Here Jupiter promises a rich, warm family life, though not always from the beginning. If there are bad aspects to Jupiter from its dispositor, the ruler of the chart, or angular planets, or if it shares the fourth house with the Moon, Mars, Pluto, Neptune, or Uranus, there may be loneliness or privation in childhood. However, the power and faith of Jupiter will succeed sooner or later in surrounding them with the love and warmth of family life.

There is a great desire to assist in making basic changes in society, helping to reform it for the good of all. Artists try to create a new way of looking at things; politicians, a new social order; musicians, new forms and style; writers, a new look at life, at love, morals, etc.

The only danger for people with Jupiter in the fourth is that they do not always aspire as high as they might, but are so content with the family and community that their goodwill and understanding can be reserved for just the inner circle, while the needs and rights of those outside are disregarded.

With good aspects, it gives a loving, giving father. With difficult aspects, the father may be too self-indulgent, or be gone on business or pleasure too much of the time, or be gone altogether, although his loss is sometimes compensated for by someone who becomes a father figure. Good aspects can indicate the inheritance of a home, land, or real estate.

Jupiter in the Fifth House

This is an excellent position for Jupiter as its powerfully harmonizing nature can work with both the Ascendant and the Midheaven to give leverage to whatever goals are set. People with Jupiter in the fifth have durable egos and are not put off by much of anything. They can rise to power in whatever field they choose. However, due to the location of Jupiter below the horizon, they may choose to become the power behind the throne; the king-maker rather than the king.

Children and young people are very important to those with this Jupiter. They may groom their children to achieve their personal goals. They are born leaders, but, until they reach the stage where their leadership is acknowledged, they may be lonely, because they are not good followers. They are usually self-employed; if they work for others, they will function best with a minimum of supervision. They may have trouble in school due to a strong sense of their own rightness and their disdain of low behavior. They feel that the mighty authority they sense within themselves far outweighs the puny authority of parents, teachers, and bosses. They have great courage and inner strength, though they may not know this about themselves until later, after they've lived a bit and examined their own lives and the results of their choices.

Jupiter in the Sixth House

Without strong aspects from above the horizon, this can be a weak position for Jupiter, not bringing the rewards from transits that come from other locations. Those with a sixth-house Jupiter will get their greatest pleasure from the work they do. Most of their good times occur in the workplace or with fellow workers. They make good managers because they are kind to subordinates and are usually loved and respected by them.

They have great sympathy for others less fortunate than themselves and may give away more than they can afford (unless Jupiter is in Capricorn). They are inclined to align themselves with hopeless or outworn causes, techniques or individuals, and may sacrifice much out of loyalty. Their politics is truly the politics of love. They are inclined to work by fits and starts, and need a well-placed Saturn and Sun to help keep them moving steadily forward.

Their line of work is very important to them. It must be valuable work, something of significant use to humanity. They cannot be happy with frivolous or purely commercial work for long.

A good placement of Mercury or Uranus is necessary to give perspective, because Jupiter here doesn't have much. If Mercury is not strong, this person can suffer some big errors in judgment somewhere along the line.

There will be more power, more follow-through, if Jupiter is in fixed signs, particularly Scorpio. There is little strength in the mutable signs for furthering self-interests, but much for helping others.

Jupiter in the Seventh House

"All for love and the world well lost." These people are total romantics, ever seeking the ideal, particularly the ideal mate. They are generous and noble toward others and expect the same treatment in return. They love to party, especially with the beloved.

Intensely idealistic, they will go to extremes to establish a just society. With Jupiter in the sixth within orb of the seventh cusp, they will work along established lines; in the seventh close to the eighth cusp, bolder, more willing to sacrifice life or reputation for a cause.

Generally, there is a lot of luck in life with this Jupiter. Often, they are too involved in self-development and enjoyment of life to work hard for a career, unless aspects testify otherwise. It is a good position for a performer, a minister, a politician, anyone who stands before the public. It gives charisma and a buoyant, self-confident appearance. Standing erect, carrying their heads high, their noble, dignified bearing gives no clue to the loneliness at the heart of this aspect, which stems from rarely or never finding anyone or anything close enough to the heart's ideal.

Generally loyal to a fault, they will never desert anyone to whom they have given their word. They are capable of idealizing groups to too great an extent, and may go to the wall for causes or individuals who don't deserve it, who don't even ask for it. There is a great deal of courage with this Jupiter, and a need to display it; usually emotional courage in a woman's chart, physical courage in a man's.

With all these noble qualities, however, these people are capable of being manipulative for their own benefit or for that of others they seek to assist. They will never back away from a conflict, but, will usually try to win through charm or politics first, turning to force only as a last resort. With difficult aspects, they may get caught at some time in a conflict of interest and be forced to break off with one cause or group in favor of another.

They are usually faithful to partners. If other aspects and events should force a separation, they will find someone new to be faithful to.

Jupiter in the Eighth House

With this placement of Jupiter, there is a deep insight into nature; wordless knowledge, and a depth of feeling, but not always the means to express it. This is a good position for a writer, a scientist, a psychologist, or a musician. It is not a testimony to worldly renown, but generally guarantees a modest success, the ability to earn a decent living in a satisfying profession. With this Jupiter, they are able to work alone and without support for years, following their star at just above survival level, if need be. They trust in the basic plan of life and nature to keep them afloat. They believe in themselves and in their purpose in life. They are capable of professing and clinging to highly unpopular views, maintaining dignity in the face of universal disbelief and scorn, knowing that the wheel will turn their way sooner or later.

They have insight into the human heart and believe that all people are trying to do right, but are limited to varying degrees. There is an awareness of the depths to which humans can sink, the terrors of the night, the hells within as well as the heavens beyond. They are capable of performing great acts of courage, both physical and emotional.

They are generally believers in God in a quiet way, or in some sort of natural higher moral authority. Politically, they are rarely revolutionary, rather wishing to reestablish old-fashioned moral values. If they become involved in political upheavals that bring them to power (at work, at home, in the community), they generally seek to maintain the status quo. With hard aspects they may even become reactionary or repressive.

They have a love of the so-called "common" people, their dreams, needs, and sorrows, but are not terribly idealistic about changing them into something more noble. They see too clearly the evil inherent on the material plane.

Given other aspects for it, this is a partial testimony to theft. They may live outside the law in some way, or, if not, they have sympathy for those that do.

Jupiter in the Ninth House

This location of Jupiter gives a powerful, lifelong upward striving that frequently results in worldly success. There is a hunger here for knowledge and experience, that seeks an outlet in reading, studying, traveling, learning foreign languages, talking to travelers, taking courses; in short, a lifelong effort to expand their horizons. Often this makes these people seem more knowledgeable and better educated than they are, as they can be too restless for formal schooling and so pick up their educations here and there as they go through life. They like to surround themselves with friends and associates who are more knowledgeable than they in areas that interest them, so that, although they may not have answers themselves, they are comforted by the thought that they know someone who does.

They are usually excellent salesmen and can sell anything or convince others of almost anything they believe themselves, exhibiting an irresistible, boisterous enthusiasm for whatever it is they are trying to sell. They appear to be sunny, generous people, whether they are or not, always ready to contribute time and money to good causes. In reality, they are master politicians, exceptionally slick at getting their own way and making others like it. They see the seamy side of human nature but find it humorous, and are good at manipulating it to their advantage. This is an excellent position for a politician, though the thrill is more in the pursuit of victory than in the administration of it afterward, so their careers may seesaw.

Philosophy is important to them. They will be at work all their lives on a satisfactory world view, which they delight in selling to others.

Jupiter in the Tenth House

This is an excellent indicator of success and enduring fame, although sometimes not until after death. It is an excellent placement for a successful career effort, although oppositions from the fourth house unrelieved by trines or sextiles can frustrate success. Usually, however, they will have achieved their career goals by their early fifties.

They will always find help, financial help from partners, or whatever they need in order to continue. In turn they are generous in manner and are given to lavish entertaining, particularly for political purposes. They are past masters at being in the right place at the right time. If they write, they find publishers; if they paint, they find patrons. Whatever they do tends to work out for them. They may or may not make a lot of money, but they will always have as much as they need to do what they want to do.

They are inclined to be greedy when it comes to gaining power, and jealous of it once they get it, ordering others about and throwing their weight around; sometimes losing the love of those who supported them initially, but clever at buying the love of newcomers. No matter how autocratic and obnoxious they become, they are always capable of outbursts of generosity, for they don't want to give up the image they have of themselves as generous and kind to those beneath them.

If life and bad aspects frustrate their ambitions, they may become bitter, though they will try to hide it. They may suffer from grandiosity, the secret belief that they are better than anyone realizes (not so secret in some signs). This position gives tremendous vitality, the ability to bounce back and snatch victory from the jaws of defeat. They are never done until they are dead, and sometimes not even then.

Jupiter in the Eleventh House

This location of Jupiter adds luck to the life. Without serious bad aspects, these people will have influential friends who assist them greatly. Even with bad aspects, this Jupiter acts as a cushion, preventing difficulties from going to too great an extreme. No matter how lonely or unsatisfactory the personal life may be, in front of groups they appear vital, relaxed and in control. It is a good position for a teacher, politician, bandleader, manager, or anyone dealing with groups. They love to party and hang out with as large a crowd as possible.

Whatever group these people lead will feel tremendous loyalty towards them, and they in turn will feel loyalty to the group. In fact, they cannot work with or for any group they don't love or believe in, which may cause difficulties when it comes to earning a living, because they hate to compromise their principles. This can dull a career effort because they will work with great enthusiasm for a while, only to lose interest when they discover faults in individuals in the group, or that the group's goals are not totally altruistic. Another difficulty is that when they do find a group they can believe in, they have a hard time leaving it for bigger and better things. Although they are so group-oriented, it is always the individuals within the group who are important to them, rather than the group itself; thus, a career soldier may hate the army but love his unit.

These people are believers, first and foremost. They need to show enthusiasm and to belong to something noble and worthy that they can be enthusiastic about. If they show cynicism, it is only a thin layer, and they will throw it aside as soon as possible. It is good for them to develop some kind of special skill or area of expertise that sets them above the common herd, at least in their own mind. Otherwise, they will suffer from a vague feeling that they deserve better than their lot. If they play an instrument, they will belong with the greats of music and be one with Mozart and Beethoven—at least while they are practicing.

Anything that enhances their membership in a group, that enables them to enlighten or entertain others, is good for them. They are usually good joke and story-tellers, and like to be the life of the party.

The closer Jupiter is to the twelfth house cusp, the less they will be oriented towards profit-making, and the more towards helping those less fortunate than themselves.

Jupiter in the Twelfth House

Jupiter in the twelfth gives a proud bearing, similar to Jupiter in the first, though there is often a touch of sadness about it, like the dignity of a king or queen in exile. These people are extremely good-hearted and willing to give and to help others, but they often suffer from a feeling of spiritual isolation, a sense of loneliness in their perception of things, the feeling that no one else shares their point of view. They are inclined to give too much to friends, acquaintances, or strangers, and then be hurt to the quick by the ingratitude, sloth, and selfishness they may get in return. This can cause them to swing to the opposite extreme and to refuse to help others in any way or to give anything at all. They may become so isolated at some point that they will require help from an institution. This often occurs through the workings of fate, or karma, and no apparent fault of their own. Nevertheless, a twelfth-house Jupiter is a potent insurance against real disaster or any lasting difficulty. It is a sort of magic talisman that does little when things are going well, but casts a protective spell in times of trouble.

The sorrows of an older relative or advisor may be a turning point for them, causing them deep anguish and introspection that leads to a change of perspective or of lifestyle.

The closer Jupiter is to the Ascendant (within ten degrees) the more benefits it brings, similar in quality to those it brings in the first house; though there will often be strings attached, or varying degrees of constraint in the ability to take full advantage of them.

ħ

Saturn Through the Houses

For thousands of years, Saturn was considered to be the last planet of the solar system—until the development of technology enabled astronomers to locate Uranus, then Neptune and, finally, Pluto. (Some think there's still at least one as-yet-undiscovered planet out there.) Saturn is one of the most interesting objects in the heavens as its equatorial ring (made up of the dust of exploded satellites, according to one theory) is a beautiful sight to anyone with a telescope, when it reflects the Sun's light at different angles. Saturn takes almost thirty years to orbit the zodiac, spending about two-and-a-half years in each sign, and moving at a rate of about one degree per month.

Thus Saturn was considered for millennia to be the ultimate planet, comparable to a judge in society, the final authority, beyond personal concerns, swayed only by abstract and absolute considerations of justice and morality. It is the negative pole of the God principle (Jupiter being the positive pole), taking away that which has been forfeited through misuse, or that is needed somewhere else to maintain the system as a whole.

Saturn is considered to be the ruler of Capricorn, not the most comfortable rulership since Capricorn stands at the top of the wheel, corresponding to the tenth-house principle of career and reputation in the community—in actuality, a difficult placement for Saturn.

However, since Capricorn is the sign located the furthest from the Sun/Galactic Center, in the area of the zodiac that is the closest to outer space, away from the galaxy, the area where winter begins in the northern hemisphere, the rulership of Saturn seems totally appropriate.

Capricorn is opposite the signs Cancer, located closest to the interior of the galaxy, where summer begins. Cancer is ruled by the Moon, the first, closest and fastest "planet," relative to the Earth, while Saturn is (or was for thousands of years) the furthest, slowest planet.

Saturn is closely related to the Moon by cycles, as in a progressed chart the progressed Moon circles the zodiac at almost exactly the same time as does transiting Saturn. Together the Moon and Saturn rule the forces of nature; the Moon is the burgeoning force that bursts the seed and pulls the DNA into external growth and manifestation, while Saturn is the focusing or distilling energy that condenses the life force down into the tiny compass of a seed that will survive the frost of winter. Even as they represent the first and last planets, the Moon and Saturn represent the beginning and the end, birth and death, babyhood and old age, animal hungers and wisdom, the limits of human existence.

The location of Saturn in a chart almost always indicates an area where there will be a constant effort required to avoid difficulties throughout life; what kinds of difficulties will be determined by sign and aspects to Saturn and its dispositor. Where Saturn is located, things will not be easy; there will be no quick results. Saturn will never let anything develop until all the necessary groundwork has been laid. It rules the principles of condensation and focusing. It rules detail; not the exquisite finishing touch of Venus-type detail, but the kind of nit-picky detail cherished by people who dot every "i" and cross every "t."

Transits of Saturn often indicate times of stress, of poor health, financial crises, or losses due to acts of nature, that are tests of the strength of a spirit. Once these transits are over, it is often found that dead wood has been swept away, leaving a clearer path to necessary goals; and, although the process may have been painful, usually one is better for it.

Saturn rules the final years of life usually beginning somewhere between sixty and eighty-four (the onset of the Saturn years varies with the individual), the years when we must cut back to some extent on our worldly activity and conserve our energy and resources. This is when, often, we are tested by ailments and loss of physical powers; when our knowledge of the world, our thoughts and memories, and our accumulated wisdom are our primary equipment.

Saturn is also allied with Jupiter in ruling finance— as Jupiter rules bull markets, Saturn rules bear markets; as Jupiter rules loans and grants, Saturn rules debts and taxes. Together, Jupiter and Saturn rule the upper limits of the human community: authority, government, society, and the officials that administer codes and mores.

In the body, Saturn rules the bones.

Saturn in the First House

Saturn rising gives a strong sense of responsibility from early in life. These people deeply crave to be taken seriously and to be respected. This usually acts as a lifelong impetus to development, the climbing of some sort of ladder toward some sort of goal, with security and respect as the prize.

There is frequently some sort of deprivation or frustration in youth, childhood perhaps not giving enough freedom to play or be with other children possibly due to the demands, fears, or needs of parents or guardians; but sometimes due to self-isolation. This can turn the fantasy energy inward, causing them to create outsized life goals, impossible to achieve.

The life will always be difficult as Saturn transits will bring tests and frustrations that must be overcome. Some will be, but not all. Saturn's sign and its relationship with other planets will give a clearer picture of the balance between achievement and frustration. If Saturn is related to its dispositor through aspects, there will be a greater ability to overcome obstacles. The tests will be tougher if the aspect is a square, opposition, or inconjunct, but the strength to survive them will be greater as well. If Saturn is not related to its dispositor, there will be considerable frustration.

This position brings much self-questioning and deep inner fears which seek resolution in external areas where they can prove themselves, mainly to themselves. If their belief in the worth of the self has been eroded by childhood failures, frustrations, or repressions, they will sometimes appear to fail on purpose; acting as their own worst enemy. They will say or do something, make some astonishing goof, at a critical juncture that will cause them to lose all or much of what they have been struggling for. A strong Jupiter and Venus are necessary to bring in the intuitional and hopeful forces of life to banish the anxieties of this powerful angular Saturn.

These people are usually capable of being highly organized, and of organizing anything they set their minds to; capable of holding a massive array of detail in mind and maintaining a realistic overview. They make good managers, but usually don't function well in the top ranks where boldness and imagination are necessary, neither of which are Saturnian qualities. With the Sun, Jupiter, or one of the outer planets high in the chart, however, they can be extremely effective administrators.

They may suffer from poor health early in life and at some point will have a serious bout with illness, or suffer from a chronic complaint, distressing though not fatal. Their anxieties frequently show in their faces. They don't fancy themselves, and find fault with their looks in youth, hating a big nose or some other feature. As often as not, though, they are attractive to others, with good bone structure that keeps them looking good in later life while others are losing their looks. In youth, they are often taken to be older than they are; in age, younger. In their advancing years, they can show strength and endurance while others their age are falling by the wayside.

Some are so anxious and think so poorly of themselves that they spend a great deal of time in retreat, fantasizing what they wish they were. Even with all this, this is a good aspect for success because it gives tremendous stamina, determination, and follow-through once the inner fears have been adequately dealt with.

Saturn in the Second House

This position of Saturn is a good aspect for success if there are planets near the Midheaven. These people take themselves so seriously that they are bound to convince others to do so as well. They may set out to do the impossible, but somehow one feels they can pull it off. They may have trouble in youth, when they suffer from the feeling that nobody is taking them seriously enough, which may cause them to demonstrate their importance in negative ways, arguing, arrogance, sarcasm, even fighting, running away, and getting into various kinds of trouble.

They want to earn their own living their own way, and although this may not happen as rapidly as they'd like, it does happen sooner or later. They crave a firm economic foundation based on their own career and lifestyle and, although this approach has its ups and downs, eventually they will achieve it. Unless other aspects show it, they are not usually big on a formal education, but instead learn as they earn, on the job.

Sexual relationships are very important to them. They are rarely promiscuous, and are not good at quickies or one-night stands. They generally seek partners they can trust not to hurt them, who take them and their needs seriously. Often they will have a sexual relationship with someone older or more socially or economically powerful, or with someone who needs them—someone they can count on not to run out on them.

Their first sex experience may be traumatic in some way, leaving them oversensitive to the possibility of coldness or rejection, or just plain afraid. This can be enough to cause them to withdraw from sexual activity altogether. When this happens, the sex drive is usually channeled into the career, giving them added impetus in that area, but leaving them frustrated and unfulfilled inside. This position of Saturn is a partial testimony to homosexuality, asexuality, or one or more homosexual experiences, usually with an older person. It can also act to delay the start of the sex life; fear of sex can keep these people virgins for a lot longer than most. It may take them a long time to become relaxed enough about sex to enjoy it—but, by the same token, once they learn how, they will probably go on enjoying it into old age.

Those with Saturn in the second frequently had to "do without" in childhood or young adulthood, and often suffer at least one major grief where they were denied some desired object or experience due to family economic difficulties. This usually contributes to their determination to take care of themselves and succeed at their chosen line of work.

They can make do with very little, coasting for long periods of time at subsistence level while they are getting their act together, but they never lose sight of the goal of having enough money to do what they want. No matter how close to the bone they may live, they will always find the means to have the things they need in order to keep developing their career skills. Being frugal with themselves, they are inclined to be a bit tight with others. Unless aspects indicate otherwise, their attitude will be the very opposite of "easy come, easy go."

Saturn in the Third House

This location of Saturn always produces deep and serious thinkers, although they may not always appear to be so on the surface. The mind goes deep, below the surface into the hidden mechanisms of life. In school they may have been considered slow, because this mind is less interested in answers than in truths. Even so it is capable of handling a vast array of details, organizing, cataloging, categorizing, putting the world view into perspective, and that includes the humdrum daily regimen. They may drag their feet over details, but are perfectly capable of organizing them once they see a reason for it.

This tendency to go below the surface of facts and symbols gives them much to say but makes it hard for them to express it. There is a great desire to express the larger realities that they perceive, but ordinary words will not do the job. If they write, they may use poetry in their effort to express what they see, or a very poetic prose. It is a good aspect for actors and painters because the added dimensions of physical performance and color give them a broader scope. The deep paradoxes of existence give them a rich sense of humor, and much may be expressed through wit.

Relationships with siblings and other children are often difficult. There may be a great sorrow connected with a sibling, relative, or neighbor child. There may be an intense and difficult relationship with an older sibling. Jealousy is usually the prime factor. This rivalry or sorrow may cause them to leave home and may affect where they settle down.

They are often overly critical of peers and slow to warm to them, which can put them at a disadvantage. Often an understanding older person will step in and help them out. There is also the danger of difficulty with neighbors. They are fearful of gossip and inclined to withdraw from the community so as to give their neighbors nothing to talk about, but this actually increases the likelihood that they will become the butt of local gossip at some point. They should find a place they like and then stay put. As time passes and people get to know them, they will gradually get a reputation as a person who can be counted on—someone of value.

There can also be difficulty with short-distance travel; keeping a car functioning may be a problem at times. There will be times when they feel stuck, unable to move. This will be eased when the mind agrees to accept the burden of detail, focusing on what must be done first, second, third, etc., as this one is perfectly capable of handling any kind of practical or organizational problem, just inclined to be slow about getting started.

With bad aspects, especially to Mercury, this position can indicate possible brain damage, retardation, etc.

Saturn in the Fourth House

This is usually a good location for Saturn. It adds weight and power to a career chart if the sign and aspects are good, giving it a solid foundation. It usually indicates a good head for business and for basic values. Sometimes it shows a highly manipulative nature—more interested in getting than in having. It frequently indicates an ambitious, career-oriented father. Sometimes a grandparent will have a strong influence on the life, particularly in childhood. Often there is some sort of deprivation in childhood, not enough love from a parent, repression, or too much responsibility put on the child too young; they may have been required to think and act like an adult too early. This can contribute to later success, but at the cost of the playful time of freedom from responsibility that should be the birthright of childhood. Perhaps the home is a poor one, causing the child shame around peers.

There is usually the desire to own land and a home with a fourth-house Saturn, but, unless aspects are very good, this may not be possible. If they are able to own land, it may be that they are not able to spend much time there, or there is some kind of loss or sorrow connected with it. There may be an element of loneliness to the home life, particularly in a woman's chart. She may live without a mate much of her life. Saturn here often makes a woman strong-minded and self-willed, inclined to go her own way and not interested in the compromises that are necessary in order to live with a mate. It is better for her to marry late so that she can be sure of what she wants and is realistic about what she is getting into.

These people are always interested in basic life values, in the fundamental realities. They are deeply serious, not given to frivolity—particularly the women, due to the relationship with the father. A heavy relationship with the father causes various responses from men depending on the sign, dispositor, aspects, etc. They may appear light-hearted or easy-going, but underneath they are very serious, as those who know them well can testify.

This Saturn is a partial testimony to long life.

Saturn in the Fifth House

Those with fifth house Saturns do well in down-to-earth, practical professions where results are immediate and clear-cut, where the practical, nuts-and-bolts nature of their creativity gets full use. It favors occupations such as carpentry, auto mechanics, farming, fishing, housekeeping, or anything where a creative response is called for by a broad range of activities.

For artists or performers, Saturn in this position tends to overly restrain the free flow of creativity, often keeping them from realizing their full potential. Exacting, perfectionistic, insecure over performance, their anxiety and desire for nothing less than perfection may prevent them from competing successfully. Their best bet will be to work in some form where they can rely on expertise with a process, such as the camera and darkroom techniques provide to a photographer, or daily practice with an instrument gives a musician, and where they can be part of a group effort, such as an orchestra, film crew, or theater company. In some cases, the creativity may be slowed not from within, but from without, by powerful, jealous competitors who stoop to unfair means. (This tendency is modified if Saturn is trine the Sun, the Ascendant, is in Capricorn, or has Venus or Jupiter as dispositor.)

A fifth-house Saturn gives a deep desire to do something meaningful, to leave something important behind. It gives great persistence and drive, but other aspects are needed to give inspiration and imagination. If these are also present, these people are capable of incredible creativity, though the results can range from the sublime (Mozart, Beethoven) to the unique (Sir Richard Burton) to the ghastly (Madame Curie, Joseph Goebbels) or nasty (William Randolf Hearst).

Competition for these people is deadly serious, whatever form it may take. They take romance very seriously. There may be an inner conflict over morals versus sexual needs. They are inclined to have at least one affair with someone quite a bit older than themselves, or at least a severe crush. They are inclined to allow ambition to affect romance, desiring a relationship with one who is, or seems to be, important, or who might enhance their status in some way. This desire is not likely to be satisfied. If they get the desired relationship, it will probably bring very different results than they had hoped. There is often a sense of loss or disappointment with romance. They may feel that they have not had as much as others, although in fact they may have had more than most. They may brood for years over a heartbreak that others would have forgotten soon after, or feel guilty over the hurt they themselves have caused discarded lovers. They tend to view fifth-house matters in much too serious a light. They need to learn to emphasize joy and gaiety; less moralizing, less judgment, fewer demands on themselves as well as their lovers.

This position of Saturn makes having children difficult. It may deny them altogether. It may bring them late in life. It may bring too many too soon, so that providing for them is difficult. One or more may be chronically ill, or die in babyhood, childhood, or youth. If the Moon, Mercury, and Saturn's dispositor are strong and well aspected, these negative possibilities will lessen. In this case, they will probably transfer at least part of their own ambitions to their children. They may expect so much from them that they are bound to be disappointed. However, in some cases the child responds to the parent's expectations and brings great pride in their achievements.

This location of Saturn gives the ability to work hard and long at something, but often not until a certain amount of inertia has been overcome. Once they are motivated, however, a momentum builds and they will keep going against all odds until they have reached their goal.

Those with a fifth house Saturn should never gamble, or at least, never more than small sums that they can afford to lose.

Saturn in the Sixth House

Saturn in the sixth gives the ability to organize, work hard, and concentrate, to appraise situations practically and realistically. They see the world and their own place in it clearly and without sentiment. There is usually a strong sympathy for the underdog, for all the little people everywhere, and a desire for their comfort and happiness. There is a deep inner need to serve humanity in some way. This need must be met to prevent the possible development of some sort of chronic illness.

Those with this placement of Saturn tend to worry a lot. The worry can't be stopped altogether, but it can be broadened to include a wider community than just the self and its personal concerns. If they can feel that they are working for the good of all in some way, they will feel themselves to be part of something real. If they don't, they will tend to feel cut off and unappreciated, and the result will probably be physical problems of some sort.

These people are very critical, most of all of themselves, and they will try hard to perfect themselves in all areas, constantly working at programs to better themselves. They tend to be disappointed with the comparatively slack efforts of others in this respect, though they usually keep this disappointment to themselves, except in the work arena.

They will probably have a difficult boss at some time. They would usually prefer to work for themselves, but have a hard time getting it together. They often have a hard time with authority figures because they are inclined to be know-it-all, preachy, or overly righteous. The cause is usually an inferiority complex. Their critical nature is rarely satisfied with their rung on the ladder, and so they are angry at themselves for not doing better and resentful of those who are.

They may develop a rigid set of high-minded principles as a bulwark against life's inequities and difficulties. This philosophy is no more than a defense mechanism and can interfere with close and loving relationships with others, coming between them and those who need their love and understanding.

Those who put their energies to work for the good of a larger group will find a great source of pleasure in the work itself, in sharp contrast to the negative feelings of an underappreciated "wage slave" they may have working for a purely commercial concern. Once working for a worthwhile cause they may stick with it for years at very low pay, glad to be out of "the rat race" and not wishing to raise uncomfortable issues of self-worth by asking for more money.

Saturn in the Seventh

This placement of Saturn can cause a variety of results, depending on the sign it is in and the aspects to it. Relationships are always taken very seriously, particularly marriage. Requirements for a mate can be very exacting; sometimes so exacting that no one ever qualifies. The mate is frequently older, more experienced, or more ambitious. They may marry primarily out of a sense of duty. Sometimes the mate is ill, or so heavily committed to another family or to a job or career that the relationship is not as fulfilling as they might wish. There tend to be difficulties with the marriage, sorrow, loss, loneliness, disagreements, separations, yet the sense of duty and commitment can be so strong that ultimately it wins out over all difficulties.

These people are very exacting of others, but equally exacting of themselves and their duty to those they love. They are always very responsive to what they see as their duty, perhaps to such a degree that it burdens their lives, especially in youth. They are attracted to ambitious people and are very ambitious for those they love and eager to help them succeed. Sometimes they feel a secret contempt for those who seem too lightweight, uncommitted, or free and easy. They tend to be a bit restrictive of those they love, to keep them on too tight a rein, or ask too much of them. If they rise to prominence, it is frequently through the efforts or ambitions of a parent, mate, or patron.

This location of Saturn tends to give physical strength, drive, and stamina, and the ability to overcome physical obstacles that would stop most people. They can work harder, faster, and longer than others, push themselves to break records, push past the herd in a physical sense, and to prove themselves in the eyes of others.

They seem to have more asked of them than most people. Because of their sense of duty and commitment, others are inclined to place heavy demands on them, which they are glad of or resent, depending on other factors, but which they will in any case struggle to fulfill.

Saturn in the Eighth House

People with Saturn in the eighth have a deep insight into nature and human nature and a fascination with death and other states of being. They often have a strong desire to save humanity, or at least some part of it. This position attracts effective advisors. It also tends to be politically conservative.

They can have a certain blindness about themselves and the things or people they believe in, with a set of fixed ideas that can sometimes get in their way. Their usual refusal to see their own stubbornness brings them many losses in life, until they face themselves and can accept the truth about themselves.

They tend to wear well and often gain in attractiveness as they age. They usually have a brush with death at some point that changes their live—either their own death or that of someone else. They may deal with death, or after-death states, in their work in some way, if there are other factors that confirm it.

These people are often very concerned with money, security, and position due to a great lack of one or all of these in youth, and will probably gain a great deal of the first two at least, though possibly never enough to satisfy. They are capable of giving gracefully, effectively, and thoroughly, when needed, whether of time, services, or material things. The sorrows of their lives can be transformed into humor; they are usually very amusing people. In youth they are often very attractive to older people who can be helpful to them. With other factors, this guarantees charisma; yet in spite of it they are often lonely. They attract others, but often not the ones they'd like to attract.

Saturn in the Ninth House

Saturn at this angle inevitably brings about some sort of moral crisis, and the worst of it is that everybody usually knows about it. If there is any sort of weakness of character, this aspect tends to hold it up to the light and magnify it for all to see.

This position is often found in the charts of those who have tremendous ambition in youth, not so much to accomplish great things as to be accepted by those at the top. Often, in their climb to the top they do not lay a broad-enough foundation to begin with, but try to get there as quickly as possible; and so, although they may reach their goal, their foundation crumbles beneath them and they don't stay up there too long.

Sometimes they are not concerned enough with the ethics of the methods they use, and this can catch up with them, usually at the worst possible time. The scandals that pursue them can be of any sort (sign and aspects will tell), but are often sexual or involve a misuse of funds, or both. They may be completely blameless, yet still be pursued by scandal. In order to overcome or survive it they must have built a very broad base of support, and this they so often fail to do. If they were poor in childhood, the danger of trouble is greater, because the temptation to take advantage of access to other people's money (or other peoples' mates, etc.) is more likely to overwhelm them.

If they achieve positions of political authority, they are often the ones forced to make hard, unpopular decisions. If not actually in politics, they may have dealings with politicians and, if so, should be wary, as they are apt to suffer from the association.

As for their own political bias, they are more likely to be conservatives than liberal, or what might better be called radical conservatives, because they are more inclined to take matters into their own hands than to set up systems. Their philosophy, whether it be deeply political, religious, or just a common-sense set of values for daily living, is generally not tremendously complex; it's fairly simple and rather strict. Black is black and white is white; good is good and bad is bad. This gives them the ability to make decisions without the agonizing that those with more complex value systems feel. Their decisions may be wrong, and later they may come to see that they were wrong; but, at the time of crisis, the issues were very clear in their minds.

Sometimes this placement of Saturn shows up in charts of those born to wealth and position, who are forced by birth to shoulder responsibilities that, given a choice, they'd rather not have to take on.

With a ninth-house Saturn, there is often a fateful connection with a foreign country or a foreigner. Aspects and the sign it is in will show if this brings benefit or harm.

These people do not like to defer to others. They will do so in order to get where they want to go, but their inclination to take matters into their own hands, while it sometimes gets them into trouble, at other times gets them into positions of authority. Thus, actors may become directors; a policeman may become the police chief; Walt Whitman, when no publishers would take his book, published it himself. As Harry Truman, who had a ninth-house Saturn, said, "The buck stops here."

Saturn in the Tenth House

Saturn at the top of the chart usually gives great ambition and desire for success, but, without supportive aspects, the negative side of Saturn makes these hard to realize. Despite their ambition, they are inclined to be pessimistic about career matters and, though they may try hard, they find it difficult to project a positive, self-confident image. Usually some situation in childhood prevented them from getting enough enthusiastic ego support from parents or teachers, so that later they have a hard time believing in themselves. If they manage to overcome this, they can go to the opposite extreme, the ego becoming too hard, too independent of input from others. The will to succeed, once it has been forged, can be so careless of others that they may turn to illegal, immoral, or violent means to achieve or retain power.

These people must be more careful than most to walk a straight line and keep their private lives truly private, because fate has a way of holding their mistakes up for everyone to see. They must take extra pains to keep their credit rating solid, repay loans on time, and so on, because the reputation of a "deadbeat," once acquired, is very hard to get rid of with Saturn at the top of the chart.

Whatever the aspects, those with this location of Saturn have further to go and more obstacles to overcome than most. Those with supportive aspects and a strong Mars can develop a machine-like momentum that will eventually drive them over all obstacles, but they will lose many friends and make many enemies in the process. They are inclined to be insensitive to the needs of others, particularly their need to be praised and encouraged. They can be extremely callous and overly competitive where career or public acclaim is involved, trampling on others in their own need to get ahead. Those who are too sensitive to go this route may just give up any attempt at a career, feeling that the dog-eat-dog world of career competition is more than they can stomach.

In any case, Saturn in the tenth house is a very difficult spot. Success is not easy and, once achieved, can be lost overnight through a scandal or power play. Even those careers that seem founded on the broadest of bases can be tarnished after death by scandal or changes in public taste or opinion. Sensitivity to others must continually be stressed.

There is usually a difficult relationship with the mother, and not enough contact with the father.

Saturn in the Eleventh House

At this angle, Saturn tends to limit the social life in some way. The circle of friends may be small, even nonexistent. Or, if they make friends easily, they may be forced to drop them at some point due to circumstance. There will be at least one incident where they get into serious difficulties through the actions of a friend or group of friends. They may get into hot water for using a friend or friends for personal gain where they should not have. In general, unless there are good supporting aspects and several indications to the contrary, they suffer more from their friendships than they benefit.

They are inclined to have a fearful, cold, suspicious, superior, sarcastic, or other negative attitude toward social groups in general, and so frequently are considered odd, cold, or unsociable, in return, though this may be modified by other factors. They usually have a childhood trauma to overcome; some situation, often at school or involving neighborhood children, where they were humiliated by, or in front of, a group of their peers. This childhood agony casts a shadow over their entire lives, making them fearful of groups and of forming friendships. Somehow they were singled out as odd, different, or not as good as the rest. This kind of experience takes a tremendous amount of heart and will to overcome as an adult, but if they succeed they can become a great force for good in the community—as long as they keep a low profile and refrain from seeking power.

They may make at least one move to escape a social situation that has become more than they can bear. They may pretend not to care about society or social power, but deep inside they care very much, and may be far more aware of it and of the social standing of their associates than they reveal. Some may make the mistake of dropping true friends of lesser social standing for others who appear to have more. This often results in a loss of standing with both groups.

These people are inclined to be clannish, to join social groups that exclude others, to become part of something that sets itself above or apart from the rest of society. They are inclined to regard attending social events as a duty and to shun organizing them. They feel much more comfortable with one or two close friends, or with family members.

If they rise to public renown, they are very sensitive to publicity, which is often hurtful to them or their careers. They are not usually overly ambitious and, if they rise to fame or power, it is usually due to fate or circumstance or the efforts of their associates rather than to their own efforts, because they generally scorn to strive for it and often hold a poor opinion of their would-be constituents. They are wise to fear power because it has a way of turning on them, leaving them high and dry, without friends, disgraced—and, in the case of heads of state, imprisoned or assassinated.

Saturn in the Twelfth House

People with Saturn in the twelfth house are extremely independent and inclined to go their own way. They were exposed to adult situations and pressures at an early age, requiring them to develop their own approach to life earlier than most. They are hypersensitive to public opinion but, at the same time, are capable of maintaining a go-to-hell attitude as a defense, which can get them into hot water, particularly in youth. They can do well in life because they have the innate organizational ability of the six/twelve polarity. Later in life, they are able to maintain an image as a perfectly ordinary person while living an absolutely unique and individual personal lifestyle.

These people see only what they choose to see. They have the ability to totally ignore what is not important to them (except with an opposition to Saturn, in which case they are forced to see both sides). Problems have a way of popping up out of nowhere, particularly if Saturn is retrograde, but this is only because the blinders of the twelfth house are on. Once they confront life as it really is, they will cease to be continually shocked by the sudden appearance of difficulties.

They are often forced to spend time in an institution of some kind, either because of mental, emotional, or physical breakdowns, or because their work takes them there. It is an excellent position for doctors. Saturn's concentrative ability gives the endurance necessary for the long education, and helping others relaxes pressure on the self.

There is a great capacity here for dedication, usually to a cause, sometimes to a group or, sometimes to just a single individual. They are usually conservative in the true meaning of the word, wanting to conserve what they hold in common with others: "Waste not, want not."

In youth, they may have a brush with the law or possibly with death.

Uranus Through the Houses

Uranus is the first of the so-called modern planets, the three outer planets, all discovered within the last two hundred years by means of scientific instruments.

From our perspective, these planets—Uranus, Neptune, and Pluto—move much more slowly on their vast orbits than the inner planets (the Moon through Saturn), and therefore are generally understood to rule large-scale and long-term changes in society as a whole, because whole generations will share the same sign positions and aspects.

Uranus rules the unusual, which is not surprising since it is the most unusual planet in the solar system.

While the other planets all have their poles more or less perpendicular to the ecliptic, the poles of Uranus are aligned *with* the ecliptic. Its pattern of alignment and rotation is at complete odds with the normal pattern of the other planets. Perhaps it is because of this that it represents abrupt reversals and upheavals. Traditionally considered a malefic, or bad, influence, it does shake up the life wherever it lies in the chart, causing changes that drive the individual either to rapid growth or to extreme and destructive behavior.

Uranus rules change; not the natural constant changes that are in the Moon's arena, but permanent changes after long-term stresses have built up, such as earthquakes in nature and revolutions in government.

It takes Uranus roughly eighty-four years to complete its circle through the zodiac, seven years per sign. Divisions of the orbit of Uranus give us the major turning points of our lives: a quarter of the way around the orbit, when Uranus squares the spot it occupied at birth, is a quarter of eighty-four, or twenty-one, the age we become legal adults. Half the orbit, forty-two years, is mid-life crisis, a time when we review our lives and feel the urge to make major changes, sometimes drastic ones. Three-fourths of eighty-four is sixty-three, the age of retirement, with all the changes that it brings. The Uranus return at around eighty-four marks the fulfillment of a complete life cycle.

Uranus on the angles gives a nervous brilliance, an intense and demanding intelligence, even genius, but often also an unstable personality given to sudden impulses and eccentric behavior that are hard to defend or explain. People with an angular Uranus definitely march to a different drummer than the majority of their fellows. Their lives are often dedicated to perfecting something for the benefit of humanity as a whole, which leaves them little time or patience for the few representatives of humanity that surround them at home and at work. Even those who have close friends and good love relationships will have times when they are distant and disinterested, and some are so cold that they can have no real friends or lasting relationships, while some are just plain cruel, or violent, or both.

Uranus is regarded as the planet of the intellect, the higher octave of Mercury, and the stronger it is in a chart, the more powerful the intellect. An angular Uranus doesn't guarantee genius, but it is a big factor. Of fifty-two great composers, well over half have Uranus on an angle, and of the genuine geniuses among this group, only Johann Strauss the Elder, Johannes Brahms, Giuseppe Verdi, and Richard Wagner have it elsewhere. Of 133 political leaders, sixty-six have Uranus on an angle, well over the statistical norm.

Uranus in the First House

Uranus rising gives an intensity to the nature that is sometimes masked by a genial easy-come, easy-go social manner; but, as close friends know, behind the mask is a restless, relentless, questioning intellect, concerned with answers to all questions on all levels. Tremendously inventive, they are the ones who come up with new ideas, new ways of doing things. They act as collectors of the needs and concerns of their day—and, out of the pressure that builds up through this continual collection come answers and ways of satisfying those needs. Whatever field they choose to work in, it will be the same.

The overpowering nature of this great planet of the intellect keeps them continually on edge and makes it very difficult for them to relax—or for anyone who lives with them to relax. The intellectual orientation of Uranus makes them head people, not heart people. They may *believe* in loving one's fellow man and may even go to great lengths to practice this belief but, without a powerful Moon and/or Venus, they will not really *feel* the love (some of the worst villains in history have this position). They are not sentimentalists—quite the reverse—and kindness and compassion are things they must learn to practice. This they often do, as they are great learners and growers and will learn much from living, reading, and thinking about life and what is good and what is not. Their contribution is of the mind, inventions to make work easier, systems to alleviate social pressures. For instance, Coco Chanel designed a new style of clothing for working women, at once practical, comfortable, and elegant. They are always radical in the true sense of the word (which comes from the Latin for "root") in that they see more clearly than others to the core of things, clearing away the accumulation of outworn methods and no longer meaningful forms, and calling for a return to basic principles.

Although they may mask their intensity with geniality, they do not suffer fools gladly and can be ruthless about putting them in their place. Often considered eccentric, particularly later in life, they continue to follow their own inner voice, doing things the way they want in a lifelong experiment with style and method. Although their means are intellectual, their methods are intuitive; often they will do things in a certain way and for a purpose that they themselves may not understand until much later.

The rising Uranus generally gives a long face with a high forehead, a wide mouth with thin lips, and very intense eyes, sometimes slightly bug-eyed, or pop-eyed.

Uranus in the Second House

Uranus is not particularly good in this position. The second house, ruled by Taurus and Venus, should be one of the calmest, steadiest sectors of the chart, an impossibility with Uranus as a resident. Uranus here brings constant uncertainty over finances and resources. Most with Uranus in the second house have at least one period of their lives when they must grapple with poverty—usually in childhood, but some in later life, and some for their whole lives. It takes very good aspects and good positions of Jupiter and Saturn in the chart to modify this. Sometimes a grinding poverty in youth stimulates these people to later effort and eventual success. Even so, there is usually no real security with it, and they remain always vulnerable to sudden reverses.

Occasionally, it gives genius in the making of money, the stress of poverty creating a brilliant wheeler-dealer whose only interest is making grand financial coups. Some are inclined to borrow heavily, gamble, or even steal in order to get what they desire, often on impulse. What is more usual is that they become so used to doing without that they come to take it almost for granted and develop a cavalier attitude toward money, giving it away if they get it, spending lavishly until it's gone, or gambling it away. It is as though through suffering over money they develop a hatred for it, and try to get rid of it as soon as they get it.

This location often gives a powerful or compelling speaking voice, making it a good indication for public speakers and singers. It is a good aspect for artists, that is, good for their art, as the intellect revels in combinations of light, form, texture, and shape. Anyone with this placement will have a highly-developed sense of style and a great appreciation for art, sculpture, architecture, interior design, and clothes, though sometimes their taste goes off on a tangent and they can be considered eccentric or, at least, extremely *avant-garde*. They are the ones who will spend their entire paycheck for a painting, or a piece of clothing, while neglecting to pay the rent.

They think a lot about sex, though with what results will be shown by Mars/Venus aspects, and other factors in their charts. Some will severely repress their sexuality, while others will go to lengths to flaunt it. If there are squares or oppositions to Uranus, watch out for explosive sexual episodes that change their lives. It is a partial testimony to homosexuality or other deviations from the norm, including sometimes a severe repression which creates an emotional bottleneck and distorts relationships with others.

Uranus in the Third House

Restless and adventurous in mind and spirit, and to some extent in body too, people with Uranus in the third tend to leave home early, and usually go away to school, or as far from home as soon as possible in order to broaden their life experience. They are usually too restless to spend any more time in school than is necessary. They tend to be romantics and idealists and, no matter how hard their experience may be, or how much evidence they find to the contrary, will continue to believe that their ideals can be found and that happiness and justice are possible somewhere, somehow, someday. They always prefer the unknown to the known, the adventurous to the secure, and as a matter of course will take chances that would frighten others—with their bodies, their investments, their careers, and their feelings.

They may have one or more siblings who cause them a great deal of unrest or worry, someone very bright and unorthodox, or very troubled, or both. If there is no such sibling, they will probably have a friend, neighbor, or near relative who fills this role, as though to teach them through experience what sorrows can come through extreme behavior. They tend to hide their problems behind a humorous, light-hearted facade, preferring that the world think of them as someone with no worries. Only their family and very close associates will be aware of their personal difficulties.

Men with this Uranus tend to have strong, muscular physiques, though not overly so. Neither men nor women with this position are inclined to put on weight, due probably to the restless overflow of nervous energy that keeps them on the move and also due to the romantic idealism that reflects in their image of themselves. They tend to stay physically and mentally active into old age, with only the barest tolerance for the natural decline of their powers.

Uranus in the Fourth House

With this Uranus, traumas in childhood affect the emotional development, though it can also be a powerful stimulus to achievement and soul growth. Generally not very happy or easy-going, they can be very hard to live with, as emotional complexes cause a lot of trouble. With difficult aspects to Uranus or Mercury, this can be a real "mental case." The less difficult the aspects and the sign location, the sooner in life they can get it together. Some form of counseling is usually helpful. Once they face themselves and gain some self-understanding, they will be much happier and easier to get along with.

They are usually outspoken to a fault, often with a sort of bitter humor, and overly sensitive to criticism. Anguish at home often causes them to leave their native turf and start a new life somewhere else. Even if they do not leave physically, they are often involved in the founding of a new order, a new way of doing something. They tend to be mavericks and insist on having things their own way or they won't participate. They wish to build a new world with themselves at the center, but this brings them much loneliness. They are often misunderstood by their associates who think them odd, cold, or overly abrupt or risqué, not seeing the warmth that is in their hearts. They are usually expressive with words, saying things in a terse, humorous style that is intended either to inform or entertain.

Women with this position are more inclined to neurosis, possibly because their field of expansion, their potential for using their emotional energies to give form to something outside themselves, is more limited in our society. There is more frustration; the emotional complexes are more stimulated and the behavior follows suit.

Although both men and women with this position have a love of young people, they have a hard time dealing with them and, although they do not wish to do so, both tend to revisit their own traumas on their children. They are powerless to stop this unless they get some therapy to help them build new response patterns.

They are attracted to those very different from themselves and often choose a partner from a very different background. Their marriage may or may not be happy, but often they will cling to the mate, happy or not, fearful of losing the one who knows them best and who must accept them as they are.

Their emotional tension can translate into a strong sexuality, which may be firmly repressed for a variety of reasons. The resulting frustration can make them irritable and sarcastic and very hard to deal with. They are always desiring someone that they cannot have. Actually, this is only one focus of a perpetual must/can't that derives from the emotional cruelty they experienced as children.

Uranus in the Fifth House

This location of Uranus usually adds charisma to the nature, giving them the power to attract others, though they seem to make no effort to do so. In fact, they may have a cold, careless, rude, or arrogant manner, but others are attracted to them anyway.

They are subject to intense love affairs that they are powerless to resist (in youth, anyway), that overwhelm them and cause them to grow and change, and that sometimes overturn their lives, destroying marriages, jeopardizing careers, etc.—though at the time, they don't care. These romances can continue for years, but there is nothing to prevent them from being swept away again later on by someone new. Because they become super-alive and creative and accomplish their greatest work and growth at such times, they can't help but welcome these episodes and though they usually wish to remain loyal, they just can't.

It is a more difficult position for a woman, as she usually stands to lose more than a man does, and is more likely to give everything to those who will exploit her or who cannot or will not commit to her or change their own lives in any way for her sake. She may be caught for years in such a hopeless affair, the worst aspect being that she craves children and can't have them, or perhaps has them and is forced to give them up.

If there are bad aspects to Uranus, children will be a problem. There will be the desire for them, but for one reason or another they can't have them; or there are children, but there are too many, or at least one is chronically ill, or retarded, or emotionally unstable, causing endless worry and grief; or they are separated from their children by divorce or some other external cause, or lose them by some disaster.

Sex is problematic. Their sexual nature is intense, but can be repressed due to a variety of factors. They may be in a situation where they can see their beloved but not have sex, causing intense stimulation/frustration. They may develop a passion for someone beyond the accepted bounds, such as one of their own sex, or some-one too old, too young, too married, too high or too low in society. Often this desire is repressed or, even if admitted, is hidden from others, sometimes from the desired one as well. If this passion is repressed, it can lead to illness or emotional disturbance. Sometimes it causes them to take numerous lovers to satisfy the sexual craving that can't be satisfied by the one desired. This frustration can lead them to try to hurt the desired one in some way. If aspects are very bad, it could mean violence. They are very hard on lovers anyway, and can drive them away with cruel humor and cold treatment, a reaction to the intensity of their own feelings.

Uranus in the Sixth House

Uranus here gives a high-tension temperament that seeks to lose itself in meaningful work. If such work cannot be found, there is danger of chronic illness stemming from frustration. They may be afflicted by nervous habits of some kind and tend to overdo on food, cigarettes, drugs, or anything that eases tension, though they are equally inclined to become "health nuts" and overdo on special diets. Sometimes they go back and forth from binges of overeating to strict regimens. Most work hard at staying in shape all their lives, though some go the opposite route and do everything to such excess that it can lead to an early death.

Exercise is of great importance in order to use up the nervous energy and keep them steady. If they have a clear-cut goal and a partner, boss, or patron they respect to encourage them, they are dynamos of energy and can accomplish a great deal. They need a way to serve humanity, but the form and the method of service may be unusual.

Although they are mavericks where method is concerned, and usually work best alone, it is very necessary to them to be working for someone who appreciates their efforts and can set guidelines for them. They are good soldiers, able to follow orders and obey logical rules, and able to give orders in turn to subordinates, but they always need a respected superior to keep them in line, or they will go off on tangents, wasting tremendous amounts of time and money on nonessential ventures just to use up excess nervous energy.

The study of yoga, especially the practice of breath control and relaxation, is an excellent means for acquiring control over this reservoir of nervous energy which, if unused, can simply jitter them to death. Positive-thinking practices are useful also, because negative thinking is very destructive to them and can make them ill.

They need cheerful, steady, work-oriented individuals around them. Nervous, disoriented, negative, or disturbed companions will literally drive them crazy.

They can work with great patience and dedication for a cause they believe in, particularly if they respect the leader, who can be too eccentric or intense for most to work for but this won't bother them at all.

Uranus in the Seventh House

These people are very intense, super-charged, high tension individuals, though often their true nature is masked by a calm, controlled exterior.

As children, they can become hyperactive or even violent through the build-up of nervous tension. If they have outlets, they become extremely goal-oriented, and whatever achievements are held up to them as desirable they will go for with sustained and unflagging intensity. It is extremely important that they not be fed negative ideas as children or they will turn them on themselves and develop a variety of fears and neuroses. Extremely willful, they need calm, patient, understanding, positive role models who can match their appetite for achievement with plenty of healthy goals and ideas.

Much of what is true of Uranus in the sixth is also true here, although here the luck in finding the right kind of direction and patronage is much greater. There is the same nervous intensity and build-up of energy, but opportunities for using it are much more likely. However, it is very important that the rest of the chart be well balanced in order for this intense seventh-house Uranus to achieve anything. If there are few or weak planets in the eastern hemisphere, they will be too much at the mercy of circumstance; if there are too few planets below the horizon or those planets are weak, there will be plenty of luck but not much real need for it. Without well-placed planets to balance it and give it weight and drive, this Uranus will give brilliant responses to passing circumstances, but be unable to maintain the continuity necessary to achieve something lasting.

Those with Uranus in the seventh respond intensely to the needs of a broad constituency while remaining free of response to nearby individuals. The needs of those near and (more or less) dear are taken into consideration and weighed dispassionately against everyone else's need. This leaves them free to accomplish much, but can give them a reputation for being cold or aloof.

They tend to steer clear of limiting emotional attachments, but when they do get involved it's usually with someone just as strong-minded and independent as they are. This makes for a difficult relationship, but oddly enough, these marriages (or partnerships) often last for a long time though they *could* end at any time as the stress factor is always tremendous. Marriage does not end for a minute their interest in other people but, as this interest is more on an intellectual than a sensual level, it usually doesn't threaten the core of the marriage. What does threaten it is their own nervous intensity, which often can't relax enough to enjoy physical give-and-take in a comfortable manner. Their best bet in a partner would be someone very low-keyed and sensual who could help them to relax them enough to enjoy life on a sensual level, but unfortunately, such people often bore them.

Uranus in the Eighth House

Very independent, those with this Uranus position think everything out for themselves and accept nothing at face value. Circumstances in childhood act to set them apart in some way from their peers, causing them to feel different or isolated, and this isolation remains with them to some extent throughout their lives. Once they have arrived at a conclusion about something, they stick with it and can be extremely dogmatic. They do not like to be told what to do and will resist authority—usually not openly, but simply by not responding. They can seem very cold, disinterested, or even conceited in companionship, though this is due to shyness or their sense of isolation, as they are usually deeply caring, especially on a one-to-one basis.

Though they can dedicate themselves to a cause and work with groups to achieve it, they rarely become members of a group and will part company with it as soon as it no longer serves what they believe to be its purpose. They hate to compromise. They want to stand at the center of whatever situation is primary in their lives and, if they cannot, prefer to go it alone. If they are able to control a situation it will be by a sort of remote control, by personal example and charisma, rather than by direct or overt efforts to influence.

They frequently present a serious or stern appearance. They could never be characterized as silly or hilarious, though they may try on such behavior, fearing they won't be included because of being thought "too serious." They have an heroic streak that will surface at moments of crisis, an ability to step outside themselves and be self-sacrificing and noble. They can also break out of their customary shell every so often and do something really wild.

Uranus in the Ninth House

Uranus at this ambitious angle can bring a variety of opposite effects. It can intensify the ambition or will to succeed at all costs, or it can turn it around, creating disdain for worldly ambition. Sometimes it brings spiritual ambition, an eagerness to penetrate the mysteries of life and death and be ready for the next world. The emotional isolation can be very great at this angle and good aspects below the horizon, planets in water signs, and a good Moon and Venus are necessary to create a warm home life and stable friendships.

There may be sorrow or coldness at home in childhood or youth. The family may break up or move away from familiar surroundings. There is a tendency for them to leave home early or to be forced out on their own before they are ready, and as they tend to lack the inner resources to reestablish quickly and easily, this remains a lasting grievance. They are inclined to maintain a cool or lofty pose, which makes it even more difficult for them to ask for help.

This position brings deep political insight which can manifest in many ways, causing some to become political geniuses, able to mastermind large scale social movements for the benefit of mankind, and some into cold-blooded manipulators for the benefit of no one but themselves, and (few, luckily) into paranoid monsters who manipulate others for the thrill of seeing them destroyed. Some will have experienced from childhood the limits of human ambition and social manipulation, and so will retreat from the world, renouncing all personal claims and social ambition. It brings a cynical attitude towards the motivations of others, an inclination to suspect the worst, or even a paranoid inability to see anything but personal ambition and cold manipulation in all actions of others.

It gives courage that can become recklessness, a tendency to gamble with things that others would hold too dear to risk. Lots of love in childhood helps to ease the difficulties this position brings later.

Uranus in the Tenth House

These people never stop growing and changing, and with Uranus at the top of the chart, the sky's the limit. This position of Uranus doesn't usually bring the erratic behavior of Uranus on the other angles, at least not once youth is past. Changes are generally planned for and well integrated into the life pattern. They tend to leave home early and are on their own as soon as possible, often due to unsettled family situations. Though bold, they are rarely reckless, and though committed to change, they are not revolutionary, but work towards it in an even and comprehensive manner, dealing with its ramifications as they develop. They have both initiative and follow-through.

Though highly intelligent, they are rarely intellectuals, and generally seek a life that fulfills them physically and emotionally as well as mentally, though their emotional fulfillment often comes more from helping large groups or humankind in general than from immediate relationships, where they tend to be somewhat rigid and selfish. They need a field where their immense energies and creativity can have full sway, and will continue to seek and change until they find it. Not inclined to the eccentricities of Uranus on the other angles, still their personality and style is highly unique and they will come to be known for it.

Their capacity for work is tremendous if it is toward some end that they believe in, and even if it is just a job that pays the bills, they tend to give it all they've got, at least for a while, in order to use up the flood of energy within.

They generally know what they want and drive straight for it, a quality that can get them into hot water in youth, though they always have the ability to talk themselves out of any trouble they get into. They tend to project a quiet, cool, unsmiling manner; aloof, sometimes even cold or withdrawn, but this is a mask behind which they are taking in everything, to be released later with intimates in floods of wit, mimicry, and wildly antic humor.

They are happiest working for themselves, and are usually quite successful in finding their own economic and social niche where wealth, power, and authority are of less concern than mobility, excitement, and creative potential, and the avoidance of boredom. They have the ability to understand and capture the popular imagination, which can bring them great rewards in the arts or in any dealings with the public.

They have a marvelous, deep understanding of human nature, which makes them excellent friends and co-workers. This, together with a sort of mystical ability to come up with the right answer or action in a crisis (like the magic tinderbox of the old fairy tale), means that they will never be at a loss.

Uranus in the Eleventh House

Uranus at this angle gives great ability, sometimes even genius, at manipulating others. There is deep and penetrating insight into the psychology of others, and an ability to work with their motives to create a network of response. Whether this will be used for selfish purposes will be shown by other chart factors. Usually, they are inclined to work for the common good and the benefit of humanity, or of a group they belong to, rather than strictly for themselves. They are good politicians, able to organize groups which inevitably turn to them as leader, though they may not seek the role, and, in fact, often resent it as it puts more stress on them than they'd like.

Generally, they do not crave the limelight and, though they like to be part of whatever is happening, don't like being center stage because it makes them too nervous. Usually, they prefer to work behind the scenes. Groups are stimulating and exciting to them, to such an extent that they can be worn out by them. They need privacy so they can rest and recharge their batteries. If they become public figures, they will go to lengths to keep their privacy secure.

Friendships are frequently more satisfying to them than sexual, marriage, or family relationships as these tend to restrict their freedom and cut into their much-needed privacy. They are excellent friends and can maintain life-long friendships although, if circumstances intervene, they have no trouble forming new ones.

They are genial and charming, diplomatic, always appearing to be interested and willing to help. They can strike up an appropriate conversation with just about anyone and can pluck lifelong friendships out of thin air. They are not so agreeable in intimate relationships, where a certain selfishness may become apparent in all but the most highly-evolved. Once a relationship becomes routine and its novelty fades, they tend to take more than they give or, at any rate, to expect a great deal in return for what they do give. They tend to take from long-term relationships in order to give to new ones, or to give to groups.

They are usually attractive, charismatic, with an understated but definite style. Although they enjoy food and frequently are excellent cooks, they rarely overeat, maintaining a trim appearance throughout life. They are excellent at giving parties and at staging all sorts of events for the pleasure and benefit of groups.

Uranus in the Twelfth House

Difficulties in childhood are apt to make those with a twelfth house Uranus into mavericks; often bright, even brilliant, but frequently out of the current mainstream of human experience. They are apt to be psychological or spiritual exiles, sometimes political exiles as well, either through choice or through the activity of enemies. They have strong ideas and opinions, which they have a hard time keeping to themselves. They see the faults in everything, including themselves, and work hard to put them right. They have great sympathy for the underdog, and, given aspects of power, can do much to bring about more just and sensible ways of doing things.

Uranus, with its clinical attitude at this angle of moral sensibility, can give them a moral blind spot so that the ramifications of their actions are not always clear to them at the beginning, though with good planets and aspects, though, they may ultimately become very sensitive to moral issues. They run the moral gamut from cold-blooded killers to the greatest humanitarians.

With Uranus in the twelfth house, there is always a moral crisis of some sort. Circumstances will force these people to study issues of right and wrong and to take a stand. If they don't, and they just allow things to take their natural course, life is going to batter them pretty badly. Some choose early, some late, but all must choose. Once they have chosen right over wrong, they are able to ride out the storm.

Their critical faculty is so strong that it can hinder their progress. They do best working for the good of some alienated or misunderstood group as their criticisms will then be of use in defense of something other than themselves; although, without several planets or angles in water signs, their approach may be overly clinical.

They have trouble early in life in discriminating properly between those companions, lovers, business associates, etc., who are good for them and those who are not, and the process of finding out which is which may take a long time and bring a few shocks and sorrows along the way.

$$\Psi$$

Neptune Through the Houses

"Whom the Gods would destroy they first make mad."

Neptune, the second-to-last planet in the solar system, takes 165 years to circle the zodiac, spending about fourteen years in a sign and traveling about two degrees per year.

Neptune sensitizes, harmonizes, and idealizes wherever it falls in the chart but, at the same time, it creates a blind spot. It makes a person very sensitive to some of the matters of that house, but blind to others (similar to the way in which blind people develop supersensitive hearing and touch to compensate for the loss of the visual sense). Practical, factual things that seem obvious to most people escape them, while they pick up nuances that others would miss. Neptune on the angles gives a great sensitivity to touch, particularly on the seventh house cusp. It may be that Neptune corresponds with the right brain, which seems to be more in touch with beauty, harmony, proportion, balance, dreams, style, melody, and rhythm, while the left brain, which is concerned with method, facts, and symbols and their accurate use, may be tuned out in those areas of the chart where Neptune is powerful.

A strong Neptune can incline one to putting the cart before the horse in a variety of ways, attempting to solve community problems before the personal ones are taken care of, biting off more than can be chewed, or giving away too much before making sure there is enough left.

Neptune's location in a chart will point to an area where one is likely to be overly optimistic, unrealistic, too romantic. There will be mistakes and false starts in this area early in life. One comes to terms with reality as experience pounds home its lessons, or one turns to fantasy rather than accept the truth, and often to abuse of those substances that reinforce fantasy. The location of Neptune will show many dreams and fantasies, but their realization will be delayed until realistic means are employed. If this realization does not occur, bitterness may come to take the place of earlier optimism and romanticism.

Neptune is commonly thought to be a higher octave of Venus, and does share some of its characteristics, such as love of pleasure, beauty, music, and perfume. However, Neptune shares characteristics with all the other planets except for three. Like the Moon, it sensitizes, fantasizes, and works primarily through the emotions. It expands like Jupiter, and like Jupiter is idealistic and optimistic, eager to give and share. It postpones and delays like Saturn, and involves one with older people and those in difficulties. It isolates like Pluto, making one feel odd, unique, alone, or unappreciated. Like Uranus, it is highly inspirational, tuning one to higher realities, though they are more likely to be artistic with Neptune and scientific with Uranus. In aspect with any of these planets, those areas that they share are strengthened.

Neptune is not so good in aspect with Mercury, Mars, or the Sun. In any aspect with Mercury, it tends to befuddle what should be clear and delay what should be immediate. In stress aspects with Mercury, it can delay the learning process, sometimes indicating learning disabilities, even retardation. In conjunction or trine, it gives the ability to learn by osmosis, to inhale knowledge out of the air, but without the capacity to retain hard facts.

In conjunction with the Sun, it generally gives charm, physical beauty, and musical talent, but it dampens the ego's strength and makes it hard for individuals to assert themselves.

In hard aspect to Mars, it can cause that soldierly planet's devotion to the moral straight and narrow to go totally haywire. Mars will try to enforce the idealism of Neptune, but its nature is so much the opposite that somehow the goal is lost sight of and very different results are achieved than were dreamed of at the outset.

In the body, Neptune is involved with the hearing process as well as the sense of smell; those senses that can replace the vision to some extent. It rules what we call the sixth sense, the intangible knowledge of things that can't be seen or proved.

Neptune works from the outside in rather than the inside out. It seeks to grasp a reality *in toto* from the beginning rather than by starting with one fact, then adding another and another until a complete picture is formed. This is why it is so often out of focus, like a camera straining for too distant a subject or too wide a field of vision.

Neptune in the First House

A rising Neptune gives an intensely compelling charisma, yet at the same time it isolates and makes them feel remote from others. They have the ability to reflect back the dreams and yearnings of others, so that others see in them reflections of themselves and crave contact with them, but they themselves feel that they stand alone behind the mirror and that no one can see who they really are. The truth is that they absorb the dreams and desires of others to such an extent that they do not know themselves who they really are. They are capable of being totally overcome by the personality of another or of being absorbed into the being of another. The locations of Jupiter and Saturn and their relationship to Neptune are all-important in determining whether they have enough perspective to be absorbed only by high-level beings. They are subject to possession on all levels and should be guarded in childhood (by psychic protection) from disturbing astral entities.

They learn rapidly by absorption but have a hard time with formal studies. They usually hate school as children (unless there is enough art and music to make it worth their while) and get away from it as soon as they can, though they may return to some specific studies later in life. They are capable of being intensely inspired by circumstances and come to rely heavily on inspiration to get them through all kinds of situations. They are highly responsive to love and kindness; to anything else they simply turn a deaf ear, so that if maligned they are inclined to retreat into silence rather than stoop to argument or self-defense. They may give an appearance of aloofness, but their close associates know how intensely warm, humorous, talkative, far-out, and even silly they can be.

They love music and need it like other people need food. They like to sing, and often teach themselves to play an instrument, though they generally feel that they are not as good as they would like to be. The truth is that they find it hard to buckle down and practice, and hate to put the effort required into learning to read music, relying mainly on natural talent and inspiration. They are usually too shy to enjoy performing.

They are natural artists and poets and will be creative and unique in anything they do. They have an instinctive sympathy for babies, animals, artists, actors, and musicians. They also work well with handicapped and retarded people. They are sympathetic to people in trouble, though they must watch that they don't pick up negative vibes that lower their own spirits and affect their health. They love to sleep and their dreams are very real to them. Sometimes they have a tendency to walk in their sleep. They usually love water and are excellent swimmers, boaters, fishermen, etc.

They are dreamers and romantics, and have elaborate dreams of glory and an amazing ability to make them come true. The only danger is that sometimes they are content to dream, or to reinforce their dreams with drugs or liquor, or to allow their sense of isolation to prevent them from getting it together.

Their blind spot is themselves. They are capable of being totally unrealistic about themselves and the roles they play with others.

Neptune in the Second House

This placement of Neptune gives sensitivity to the environment. They are inclined to see the environment as a whole, and how society is molded by it, and therefore are deeply interested in social improvement and environmental protection. They have a great love of nature and the outdoors—animals, birds, trees, and particularly lakes, rivers and the seashore. They will often give up the conveniences of urban life in order to live more closely with nature.

Often, these people are attracted to a basic natural lifestyle. They are inclined to take the broad view of life, and may have some difficulty focusing on immediate specifics. They are not inclined to stick to one thing, and generally take things as they come. They also have a tendency to be super-independent, and have a hard time compromising when they believe themselves to be right.

They make good scientists or technicians because they can easily absorb the basic concepts of physics and chemistry. Generally "handy" around the house, they are able to figure out what to do to fix things. Rewards come on or near water, with perfumes, oil, in the entertainment industry (music, film, theatre), or in non-profit work for a cause.

They are very sensual and are likely to be over-whelmed by attractions to others from time to time. They in turn are usually very attractive to others, but often lack interest in those they attract. They tend to idealize or romanticize sexual relationships, while real intimacy may fail to live up to their expectations.

Sometimes, Neptune here can postpone a sexual relationship, leading to long engagements, or postpone the consummation of a marriage. Sex may seem gross to the delicate Neptunian sensibilities. It is a partial testimony to homosexual relationships; but, if so, most likely it is more of a childish, sentimental desire for the innocent love of a pal and hasn't much real sex in it.

Neptune in the Third House

Neptune here gives a deep love of the environment, or of one aspect of it, such as animals, birds, plants, or even one particular animal, one special tree, one favorite river. There is usually a love of people as well, particularly children or young people. The third-house Neptune gives a sort of Peter Pan attitude toward life, which, along with a youthful zest for life, also brings a continual state of disillusionment with individuals, groups, or everything and everyone in general, an attitude which can be surprising to their more sophisticated friends.

They are usually entertaining companions with a talent for enhancing the passing moment in any number of ways. Usually they have a gift for making people laugh, either through wit or antics (or both). This is a good placement for painters, dancers, comedians, writers, and musicians; particularly bandleaders and conductors.

Although they are highly sensitive to the emotional tone of their companions, they are strangely blind to what others think of them and don't ever see themselves as others see them—or even try to—and can be persistently guilty of some very peculiar aberrations of what most would consider obvious good form.

If there are bad aspects to Neptune, they may have a learning disability, or a brother, sister, or close neighbor with a severe health problem or learning disability. If so, they will learn much from this person.

They are attracted to musicians and artists and like to hang out with them. They may even marry one (or two). Unless they have a strong and well-placed Saturn, they are inclined to waste time in meaningless socializing or too much partying. This may be partly due to the disillusionment they feel when they try to deal with others in a business way.

Neptune in the Fourth House

*"In our little dream house we'll always contrive,
to keep love and romance forever alive...."*

People with Neptune in the fourth often find it difficult to establish a home of their own. They may not take seriously the need for a home of their own, or it may take them a lot longer than most people to get around to it. They may live much of their lives with family, friends, or in a roommate situation, particularly where it means they do not have to pay rent or take much responsibility for upkeep. Even when they do desire to have a place of their own, circumstances of one kind or another may prevent it or they may spend many years, sometimes even their entire lives, dreaming of an ideal home environment that is way beyond their circumstances.

The early home may have been chaotic in some way, and they may not have had their own space or much real privacy. In any case, privacy is very important to them, and they will put up with a great deal of discomfort to have it. The ideal home environment will be located near trees and water and be filled with plants, pets, works of art, and interesting and unusual objects from far-away places.

The father may be an artist of some sort, a sailor, an actor, a doctor, or a fisherman. He may be a humanitarian, highly sensitive, and religious. He may also be an alcoholic, and/or chronically ill. He may not be strongly committed as a parent, or may be gone from the home much of the time—even gone altogether at some point early in life. Whatever the cause, there is often the feeling that they never got the chance to get as close to their father as they would have liked.

Sometimes there is some secret fear or horror connected with childhood, something they cannot ask about or talk about with anyone. They are apt to feel as though they don't fit in with their family and childhood environment, and they may leave home early to find surroundings where they feel more at home. This search may last quite awhile; sometimes for their whole life. Sometimes it works the other way, and they remain overly dependent on the family and childhood environment, postponing departure from the nest for years. They may remain overly dependent on a parent, usually the father. Sometimes this tendency is transferred to another parent figure, such as a boss, husband, wife, uncle, or similar figure.

They are usually lovers of nature and wilderness and are drawn to scenes of natural beauty. They may feel truly at home only when surrounded by trees, plants, animals, water, and so on. There is a yearning to live immersed in nature, and to that end, they may live for awhile in a primitive set-up of some sort, such as a shack in the woods, or in a tent with no running water. They are inclined to take in strays and ne'er-do-wells and may suffer at some point from taking in the wrong person or people, or from living in circumstances where they have little say over who goes and who stays.

Neptune in the Fifth House

These people are idealistic and romantic to a fault, and are not at all realistic in their choice of lovers. They are inclined to fall in love with someone who is out of reach in some way, or someone who embodies a dream for them, because of what they do or their environment, without allowing themselves to perceive who they really are. They are capable of waiting for years for an impossible romance to materialize.

This position inclines towards sexual extremes: none at all, or too much, or peculiar tastes and attractions. It is a partial testimony to homosexuality. It can also indicate impotence or frigidity.

They are capable of great inspiration, but may rely too much on it and not enough on hard work. They are inclined to focus on the wrong aspect of things and not see the forest for the trees. They are prone to emotional instability unless there are strong, good aspects against it. They are also inclined to be psychic; but for this, too, contributory aspects are necessary.

These individuals are magnetic and charismatic but, unless other aspects are good, they may not know how to use this gift and may do more harm than good to those they attract.

This is a good position for artists, writers, or creative workers of any kind, especially those who work alone. They may suffer from a too-intense sensitivity that blocks them from fully appreciating or understanding those around them. They may feel themselves to be misunderstood by others, while it is they who do not understand others. They can be cold and callous to friends and family, tuning them out while focusing all their concern on the one they desire, who is often someone who is totally out of the question. If they do achieve union with the desired one, the romance takes a long time to wear off.

Neptune in the Sixth House

This position is excellent for musicians, members of the medical or service professions, or people whose work involves water, boats, or fishing. Anyone else will be troubled by spells of unemployment or the inability to locate the kind of work they want or even to figure out what it is they want to do. They tend to have a too-idealistic attitude towards work; and to stall around while they keep looking for the perfect job, which can't be found. Jobs that sound good often turn out to be something very different.

With the sixth-house Neptune there is a great desire to benefit humanity in some way, but too often they lack a realistic plan or the training and financial backing necessary to accomplish their goals. They must learn to start at the beginning and get training of some kind, then build on it, or branch off later. They are also inclined to hire or work with underprivileged or handicapped people, which is good when done in a pragmatic way, and their idealism is tempered with realism. Difficulties with work can result in mental or physical breakdowns. This can actually be beneficial when it forces a reexamination of attitudes and priorities.

In general, these people are inclined to give too much of themselves in the work arena and become disillusioned and discontented when they see themselves getting little or nothing in return. They must learn to keep their emotions and ideals separate from their jobs, and to be as coldly realistic as they can about what is possible and what isn't with regard to work. They should learn never to mix business with pleasure, and if they must allow their emotions to impinge on their work, to be careful.

Nine times out of ten, physical problems will be emotional in origin.

Neptune in the Seventh House

This position of Neptune inclines toward self-dramatization. They see themselves as heroes of fiction, living through dramatic events. It is very hard for them to see themselves clearly, to perceive what it is they mean to others. They continually strive to be heroic and play their roles to the hilt but, until they have a clear idea of what their roles should be, they often fail and then suffer terribly from their own sense of failure.

The ordinary roles of child, student, mate, parent, and worker are dull to them. They seek to spice them up with other considerations and, as a result, can make their lives, and the lives of their friends, families and co-workers, chaotic. They are frequently attracted to those who inspire their romantic fantasies. They are never practical about relationships, always preferring romance and excitement to practical concerns.

As they seek to play a heroic role in a partnership, they may find themselves giving far more than they are getting. If Neptune is in a fixed sign, they may continue this role to the finish. If in a cardinal or mutable sign, they will probably tire of it at some point and seek a more balanced relationship. Their romantic cravings can get them involved in some very peculiar emotional and/or sexual situations, from which they may find it very hard to extricate themselves. They tend to think of themselves as heroically independent, one who gives and doesn't need, but they desperately need clear-sighted, inner-directed people to work with and for, to keep them in balance and aimed at a goal, or else they lose momentum and lose sight of priorities.

They will throw themselves into projects, get tired when things don't work out and just let them lie, then go back to them when their enthusiasm returns. This off-again on-again approach means that their plans take a long time to develop (if they ever do). They are inspirational to others and can be of use by cheering them on, encouraging others to do right and develop themselves, but they themselves often set a poor example by their fluctuating energies and enthusiasms. They can do very well if tied in with an individual or group that is practical and down-to-earth and can keep them moving forward. Their great contribution to any enterprise is their innate optimism and ability to inspire others.

Neptune in the Eighth House

These people are often good with money, capable of gaining it through gambling, investing in the stock market, or through luck or intuition; though they are usually better at making it than keeping it, being inclined to lose it through neglect, ignorance, or being taken advantage of, rather than through overspending. They are inclined to be very tight with money, and then lose it through peculiar circumstances. This position can promise inheritance, but aspects must be very good for it to come through. The money may be less than expected, or take so long to materialize that it isn't worth it in the long run.

Early loss of a loved one or a brush with death can cause them to develop a sober philosophy of life. Sometimes this Neptune position indicates an early death, or an unusual death, or both; though, again, there must be other factors that reinforce this for it to be a serious consideration. It is dangerous for these people to drink or take drugs, as it could prove fatal.

The father often has a heavy influence on the life. Either he dies young or leaves the home; or he may be an embarrassment in some way. Sometimes he is too much of a hero, making it difficult to follow in his footsteps or, for those seeking a male partner, to find someone who can live up to his standard.

There is generally a fascination with politics or religion. Politics is not usually fruitful unless other political aspects are very good. It is hard for them to muster sufficient support to create a solid political base. If it is there for awhile, it may fluctuate or erode. There is a shy-ness, an inability to reveal the true self here that makes the self-exposure of politics difficult.

Religion interests them, but they generally have their own personal philosophy and find it hard to join a group. Although they would like to do so for the social aspect, doctrinal differences get in the way. There is a loneliness to this position. There is a craving for com-munity and family life, things that unfortunately often elude them. There is an element of self-sacrifice here as well. They may give up money for love, or love for money. Somewhere along the line, painful sacrifice will be required.

Dreams are real to them. They get important mes-sages through dreams. They may see ghosts, see things on the astral plane, or experience ESP in some way.

Neptune in the Ninth House

A ninth-house Neptune brings great dreams of glory in youth. They may dream of a career as a performer, politician, Show Biz personality, or the like, but other aspects are needed to make it happen. There is a great yearning to rise high, to make an impression on their community, audience, or constituency, but rarely do they succeed to the extent that they'd like. If they go into politics they tend to get stuck on the losing side. There is more likelihood of success as a performer, especially a singer. This position usually gives a good voice, both for speaking and singing.

Those that are withheld from action will feel great frustration; the inability to take a brave stand or to do bold deeds can contribute to emotional problems and, if other factors indicate, there can be drinking, suicide attempts, or violent outbursts of one kind or another. With supportive aspects they eventually learn to accept life's disappointments, and become philosophical about their own limitations.

They like the wide-open spaces, the sun, the great out-of-doors. This is an excellent position for anyone working in films or show business, for merchant mariners, workers in the oil industry, salesmen, or others who have to travel long distances in the course of business. They are inclined to fall in love with another country and to desire to live there. If they can't live there, they will vacation there as often as possible and, while at home, try to live in the style of the desired culture.

Neptune in the Tenth House

This is the ultimate Neptune location for politicians and performers. It is also excellent for ministers, counselors, doctors, nurses, political scientists, philosophers, artists, and entrepreneurs of all sorts. It gives great powers of charm and charisma, though rarely as intense as they'd like—though, in certain cases, more than they can handle (Howard Hughes). They usually have good instincts for what will sell. As performers and politicians, they are usually very attractive and tend to age gracefully, keeping their powers strong and maintaining a hearty image until late in life. As writers or artists, they generally leave behind a considerable body of work. As scientists, they tackle immense ideas.

They like language and enjoy using it, sometimes getting very salty or slangy. Women with this can be very sharp-tongued and pointed in their speech. These people don't usually like to stay in one place for long. They are not stay-at-homes. Frequently, they will have ties in two or more places quite a distance from each other, which necessitates constant traveling back and forth. They usually enjoy boats and fishing as a sport for relaxation.

Instinctive healers, they have a strong inner knowledge of what will help another to health, happiness, and fulfillment. They are often willing to give a great deal of time to causes or individuals they believe in.

Neptune in the Eleventh House

This is a good location for Neptune. The imagination is put to work for the good or pleasure of the group. Extremely creative, these people are inclined to put their creative energy to work on whatever arises. They are creative but, at the same time, practical, interested chiefly in efficiency and results. They are often desirous of helping or entertaining groups, but apt to be somewhat blind to the needs of individuals.

Inclined to challenge authority in youth, they usually settle down later to more effective ways of changing, dealing with, or using "the System." Women with this position of Neptune are inclined towards a career, towards making their own destiny and not relying on others, even though they may marry and have children.

Although shy in youth, they generally work hard to overcome it, developing a pleasant or entertaining social personality based on what they like in others, though some stay shy into adulthood.

These people are good at realizing dreams and are capable of long-range planning in order to achieve a desired position in life and then maintain it. They have great inner reserves of resourcefulness. They are not inclined to give up on something once they've gotten into it, and are capable of turning out a considerable body of work over many years.

Sometimes, they can be guilty of a lofty, authoritative, or abrupt attitude that can irritate others. They are unique, with their own style and way of doing things. Sometimes considered odd or eccentric, especially in youth, more often than not they are able to sell others on their way of doing things.

Often, they do their best work late in life or get into their life work late. This placement is a partial testimony to long life.

Neptune in the Twelfth House

These people are generally shy and reserved and don't seek the limelight, though they are poised and graceful when they must step forward in order to accomplish goals. Tender and understanding of human sorrow and frailty, they have a deep desire to help. With difficult aspects, their childhood home may have been unstable in some way, although there may have been a lot of love.

This is an excellent position for an artist, songwriter, playwright, or anyone who lives by capturing the needs and trends of their time. It gives a good sense of rhythm and timing.

Generally, twelfth-house Neptune gives charisma with an appearance of pride and a head held high. They tend to be naturally modest, but keenly feel their own worth, and as such, superior to the common herd. However, they remain deeply vulnerable to loneliness and are sometimes hard put to find a way out of it, as they cannot be content with just anyone as a companion. Though they are generally warm and loving, they may hide it behind a cool, reserved exterior, or tough guy pose.

They are not inclined to be go-getters unless other aspects promise it. They are more likely to let others come to them, which they generally do, though it may take time. They are inclined to have but one relationship at a time and are not into playing the field, even in youth. This position is a partial testimony to homosexuality, if only for the need for one strong relationship, and the tendency to accept what comes rather than to seek it out.

Usually, they are deeply religious, with a philosophy based on humanistic values. They are inclined to be somewhat passive and fatalistic. Often, there is an awareness of other levels of life, of life after death, or an ability to see beyond the veil. Also, there is an ability to see life in greater perspective than most, the grand panoply in which each has a part to play.

♇

Pluto Through
the Houses

Pluto is the last planet in the solar system, or at least, the last that has been discovered so far. It lies far beyond the orbit of Neptune at aphelion, and actually circles inside the orbit of Neptune at perihelion. Pluto takes about 250 years to make its orbit, spending an average of twenty years in each sign. It is about half the size of earth, much smaller than the other outer planets. Its orbit is tilted at a much greater angle to the plane of the ecliptic than any of the other planets, so that it spends a much shorter time in some signs and a much longer time in others. It was discovered in 1931 as a tiny speck in highly-magnified photos, after perturbations in Neptune's orbit indicated to astronomers that there must be another planet beyond Neptune. The years since its discovery have brought some understanding of its nature and effects to astrologers.

Pluto is very similar in action to the radioactive heavy metals that were discovered at about the same time. Its energy is deep and hidden wherever it lies in a chart, but if too much pressure is applied to it by aspect, a chain reaction is set off—and then, watch out! Experiences related to Pluto will build over a long period of time, years usually, and the crisis, if it comes, will be prolonged and exhausting, changing the life permanently, and the rebuilding process will take a long time. Its influence is best when it is distributed throughout the chart via aspects. If unaspected, or badly aspected, its tendency to isolate will collect its energy into one area of life experience, and then into one overwhelming event. It is always a factor to take into consideration in a death chart.

Pluto on the angles is difficult. It usually indicates a somewhat intransigent individual with some hard lessons to learn. It is most comfortable in the more silent and passive areas of the chart where it can remain hidden and where, if it brings on a crisis, it will not be so likely to be public. It is more comfortable above the horizon, where its energy interacts more freely with the universal subconscious shared by all. Above the horizon, it can work with others below the conscious level; below the horizon, it tends to isolate.

Pluto is said to rule mass movements of all sorts, both good and bad. Uranus may have ruled the beginning of the French revolution, but certainly it was Pluto that unleashed the bloodbath that followed. It rules mass murders, gangs, the Mafia, all secret militaristic organizations such as the CIA and the KKK, genocide, venereal diseases, plague, and leprosy—in short, a veritable Pandora's box of nasties.

Is there anything good about Pluto? Of course. There is nothing in nature that is purely bad; all have an important purpose. In the birth chart, it will force people to do things their own way, even if they'd rather not. Wherever it falls in a chart, there they must follow their secret star, often alone and in silence, in fear and trembling, with no one to guide them. At the end of life, it is often this Plutonian experience that remains the most meaningful thing that they have done, or that has happened to them. This process of change by means of quantities of small changes through the lives of individuals eventually results in the growth of civilization; out of the swamps of the brontosauri into the thrilling possibilities of a truly humane society in the future, dedicated to the good life for all.

Pluto in the First House

These people are always intensely themselves, possessing little or no power of compromise with community, family, or society. Generally, they are attractive, often emanating a strong but somewhat disturbing kind of sexual charisma. They must be careful of attracting dangerous types.

Pluto rising can bring strong sexual attractions that contain a destructive element; sexual partnerships may bring them grief in one form or another. This position is also a partial testimony to homosexuality or peculiar sex experiences.

Pluto rising people are inclined to take dangerous risks, sometimes to the point of being self-destructive. With hard Mars or Uranus aspects (or Mars or Uranus in fire signs), they can have a volatile temper that explodes periodically into rage. They are highly demanding of partners and not given to compromise themselves. They are inclined to marry someone very different from themselves and, because they resist change themselves, their marriages often don't last.

They act independent, as though they can and will do as they please no matter what, yet often they are really extremely dependent emotionally and financially on family, mate, or friends. This is something they can't change as long as they will not acknowledge it and continue to insist on their own independence in the face of all evidence to the contrary. This may be doubly hard to take because they do not refrain from making wise remarks; they generally allow their sarcasm to run rampant.

Their pig-headedness brings on difficult situations, which can force them to think, and ultimately to grow from bitter experience. They are extremely tough, as difficult to destroy as to change. They have tremendous powers of survival in spite of the crushing weight of difficulties they bring down on themselves (and on friends and family) though sometimes they manage to get themselves done in, usually in some horribly dramatic fashion.

They are fascinated by human limits, curious about others and the forces that lie beneath the surface, but not particularly interested in lending any support. They will work for causes, but usually alone and in their own way, and often by some form of destructive sabotage or non-compliance. Unless there are other strong planets involved, Pluto rising people often find it hard to act, hard to make necessary moves, hard to be on time. They see things very differently from most people, and this makes them silent, or witty and sarcastic, but rarely up front with their true attitudes.

Pluto is a deeply internal influence. Even on the angles, only intimates are usually aware of its full effect. The effects of Pluto rising may not be apparent to anyone but those who are closest to them or who have to work with them.

Pluto in the Second House

Sex is the force that individualizes these people. It brings experiences that enable them to grow. It will be the road to power for some, and for some the road to despair and ruin—aspects will help to indicate which. They know this instinctively and therefore may fear sex and attempt to repress it. Almost always, they are very cautious with it, attempting to conceal its effect on them. They possess a compelling sexual charisma that does not always attract the ones they want. They may attract dangerous types or people who are not good for them, or who take advantage of them.

They are apt to be sensualists and love good food, wine, and comfortable, attractive surroundings, including attractive companions. They are compelled into situations by their sexuality. Yet, at the same time, they are afraid of it, so they are liable to ignore, frustrate, or repress it, and this can cause them to take odd turns. They may turn to alcohol or drugs to relieve the pressure. If the sex drive is heavily repressed (as indicated by hard aspects to Saturn), their natural sensuality can turn to obsession, S & M, cruelty, or hysterics.

This is a good aspect for artists and writers, since these activities give a creative outlet for a sensuality that can be dangerous if given free rein, and equally destructive if repressed. They make good generals as control of sexuality is a necessity of army life, and sexual repression a source of power, and they instinctively know how to channel their own repressed urges and those of others.

They are often sexually attracted to those who are forbidden in some way, those of a different race, much younger, much older, married to someone else, or who come from a more primitive, less-educated or less-cultured background, or who gamble or are violent. They crave the excitement of the unknown at the same time that they fear it.

They will be much happier if they can accept their sexuality and allow it some freedom. They will be healthier and less liable to personality and emotional problems. Unfortunately they are inclined to go to extremes and so if they don't repress it, they may flaunt it. It is best if they channel it into art, painting, sculpture, music, or writing.

They can get involved with illegal, immoral, or dangerous methods of obtaining income, or become involved with someone who does. Although in general they are not highly acquisitive, pretty much taking what life has to offer without asking for more, they are capable of conceiving a passion for some object (or person) and going to great lengths to acquire it. It is wise for anyone with Pluto in the second to be cautious about maintaining accurate records because they are vulnerable to tax audit.

Pluto in the Third House

This position affects the ability to communicate, especially with peers. If there are other indications of mental instability, this will add to it. Communication can be felt to be dangerous; there is a fear of publicity, of being revealed, a fear of exposing oneself through communication. There may be a fear of travel or a fear of getting lost.

These people are easily caught up in intrigues, or are afraid of being caught in them. Their peers may think they are odd—too intense, perverse, overly secretive—which may be true, but may only be due to their difficulties in communicating.

Difficulties in communicating with peers and the community in childhood may drive them to leave home early and seek a more congenial environment, though this rarely works. Difficulties with siblings may be the prime motivating factor. There may be a sibling (or siblings, or neighbors, or associates) who bring them sorrow by living dangerously; either through an unconventional lifestyle, by having underworld connections or illegal financial dealings, or through association with underground political organizations. The worst aspects may indicate a sibling or close associate who is chronically ill or insane, or who is killed accidentally, or murdered.

Early difficulties with communication may cause them to hold back and keep their thoughts and feelings to themselves to a great extent, then pour it all out to one who seems tolerant and non-judgmental; but if their choice of a confidante is poor, they will be in worse trouble than before.

This position seems to restrain all forms of communication. Out of ninety-two writers in a sample, only four have it: out of 145 performers, only five. It gives a rich fantasy life, adding greatly to the ability of the imagination, but this is mostly non-verbal and subliminal. It is good for writing poetry (of the four writers with this position, two are poets), for casting ideas and thoughts into images, but it is difficult for publication as their anxiety over publicity keeps them from doing anything that might reveal too much to the public. There may be some justification for this, because with this position of Pluto, they are vulnerable to slander.

It gives an awareness of the dark, subliminal levels of the mind, an understanding of the animal in man, of herd psychology, of the dark forces that civilization seeks to check but that break out and cause much of the irrational behavior of humanity, both in individuals and in groups. Consequently, there is a great ability to manipulate others by means of playing to unconscious, compulsive drives. They are often attracted to macabre fantasies, science fiction, etc.

There may be dangerous, difficult, or amazing occurrences while traveling. Traveling should be approached with caution. People with this location of Pluto probably should not pick up hitchhikers. There may have been a traumatic early life experience connected with school, playgrounds, a sibling, or playmates.

They are fascinated by non-verbal communication, by words as symbols, and by the growth and structure of language, but not so much by the ordinary use of words to communicate thoughts or information.

Pluto in the Fourth House

This placement of Pluto endangers the home or the happiness of the home life in some way. If Pluto is in a fire sign, there is danger from fire; in air or water signs, from storms; in earth signs, from bankruptcy or other money troubles.

This is also one indication of an early or violent death. There may be violence or danger in early life. There may be disputes within the family that erupt into violence, or threaten to. The father or another relative in the home may be violent, revolutionary, or in trouble with the law. The life of the father may be threatened. He may be imprisoned or exiled, be in hiding, suffer racial discrimination or social ostracism, or be connected with the underworld.

The family may be broken up, lose their home, suffer bankruptcy, etc. Without several bad aspects to Pluto in the chart, it is probable that nothing of the sort will actually happen, but the threat of such things may add stress to the early life that affects the adult life to a great extent. It can cause them to be fearful of putting down roots, of establishing a traditional home and family of their own, or of being held prisoner by family responsibilities.

Those with this position are usually revolutionary, in their thinking if not in actual activity, and if not openly, then quietly, striving in some way to reform civilization from the ground up. Pluto in the fourth is deeply philosophical; early life difficulties start them thinking over the great imponderables of existence at an early age. They are students of life and see more clearly than others how individuals are parts of a whole and how each one is related to the rest through a vast network of cause and effect. They may see this in a dark light—the individual crushed in the machinery of social existence—or it may strike them as funny. Some will choose to fight the system; some to back away from it, to create a safe existence as far as possible from the mainstream.

This position tends to make a person shy, not eager to jump into the limelight. If they do rise to prominence due to other factors, they will always carry Plutonian vibes with them that can never be completely hidden. Although, in reality, they may be the sweetest and mildest of humans, with a stress aspect or two, their public image will cast the shadow of the revolutionary, or the lone wolf, or one who is prone to violence or madness, or a denizen of prisons, brothels, or mental institutions; as one who will not hesitate to use force, one who will cause permanent change, or who threatens to do so by their very presence.

Pluto in the Fifth House

This is a fairly good place for Pluto, especially when it is trine the Ascendant. These people are intensely creative. They must have healthy outlets for their creative impulses or they will go bananas. It is an excellent position for painting, writing, or for any field that provides a creative outlet. The imagination is fertile, constantly responding to external stimuli. They will not be able to buckle down for long to a routine job that leaves them little latitude for creativity, and will willingly undergo all kinds of struggles to maintain their creative independence. They rarely can accept anything the way it is; they will work to make changes of some sort. Generally handy with tools, they will continually be making changes to their environment. They are always ready to do their part to make positive alterations to the social and economic structures of their community, experimenting readily with new methods.

They have extremely sensual and passionate love natures which they become very adept at keeping on ice, so that even those closest to them may not realize this about them, thinking them cool, dispassionate, even cold. Indeed, they may not even realize it about themselves until circumstances trigger an outburst. They are attracted to Plutonian types and will have at least one painful or even traumatic romantic/sexual episode with such a one that makes them cautious from then on. They are capable of burning with desire for someone for years without showing any sign of their passion. It is rare that they do not marry, often quite early. Marriage is always the culmination of a passionate soap opera type romance, but marriage is not the end, for if romance dies out of the marriage, they will become involved in another. This in spite of the fact that they may do their best to fight it, as romantic intrigue frightens them as much as it attracts them. Sexual attractions can become obsessive, and they must learn to steer clear of hopeless involvements as the power of Pluto, if dammed, will bring terrible emotional anguish.

They are good teachers. Due to their innate understanding of subliminal emotional levels and their ability to communicate non-verbally on these levels, they have a talent for dealing with difficult, unhappy, or disturbed individuals and are often able to assist them in achieving breakthroughs and releasing their own intellectual/creative powers.

They are strongly attracted to children and will usually have their own. If for some reason they can't, they will find a way to be with them. Being in the presence of children increases their subliminal creative energies.

This placement is a partial testimony to unconventional sexual attractions of all kinds which, if repressed, will cause a variety of psychological problems.

They may seek power as a wider range for their creative energies to graze on, but they often have such a struggle maintaining control over themselves that their lives never reach that point.

They are inclined to be perfectionists in all they do and, whenever they are hard on those they love, it is usually their perfectionism at work. They *may* learn through loss not to be as demanding of others as they are of themselves.

Pluto in the Sixth House

Pluto at this angle makes what they do for a living extremely important. As long as they are not doing what they really want, painful situations will develop on the job that will force them to leave it. Often it takes them a long time to figure out what it is that they really want to do. There is a tendency to be afraid of the true calling, or of some factor in it, danger, publicity, lack of family or community acceptance, low pay, that makes them shrink from taking the plunge. Often they are finally forced into it by extreme circumstances of one kind or another. This may be why this position is not usually an indicator for career success (though certainly it didn't stop George Washington or Henry Ford). Their work must be a true *calling* or they will go to pieces on the job, exhibit extreme laziness, get sick, freak out, have accidents, etc. They may need vocational counseling to help them to focus on their true interests and abilities.

Once they have found their calling, or callings, they become extremely hard workers. Their products and methods are generally unique, and sometimes misunderstood—but if it is the thing they are meant to do, extremely necessary to the community, as they will see later on. If they do not obtain intelligent counseling early in life, they may develop bad work habits and negative attitudes toward work itself that are very difficult to change later and which can hamper their progress. If this happens, they should seek counseling.

They can be hypochondriacs, paranoid about their physical condition, but usually they are healthy above the norm. They often are interested in health and natural methods of healing.

Pluto in the Seventh House

This location of Pluto adds power to the chart, but makes for difficulty in marriage. It may deny it unless other planets are in the seventh, Pluto is in the sixth on the cusp of the seventh, or in the seventh close to the cusp of the eighth. A career partnership or other kind of partnership may be so involving that there is no room for any other kind. The career or calling may absorb them to such an extent that there is no time for marriage.

Often they choose one who is not free or not capable of marriage for some reason, or who doesn't return their interest. It is partial testimony to homosexuality, or to asexuality, impotence, frigidity, or other sexual difficulties that may prevent marriage or complicate it. If they do marry it may not last. If it does last, it will be because the partners accommodate themselves to their difficult relationship for social or economic reasons. Marriage or love relationships have an element of danger. They may become involved with someone who is troubled or who brings grief.

These people are capable of being quite blind to close associates and partners, seeing only what they want to see, convincing themselves while in love that the other is wonderful beyond all possibility and then, when the glow is gone, that the other is horrible beyond all imagining. They are capable of being extremely manipulative, cold, cruel, and sometimes even violent toward partners. This may be due to mistreatment, coldness, cruelty, or other abuse from parents or a parent in childhood. There is an urge to punish, to make others pay for what they themselves have suffered, or think they have suffered.

All of this is eased and modified by trines and sextiles, particularly to the Sun, the Moon, and the rulers of the Ascendant and the Sun's dispositor; but the likelihood of strife is increased by hard aspects.

Pluto in the Eighth House

This is probably the best placement for Pluto, its natural sector, as its subliminal nature works best in the hidden and silent area of the eighth house. It gives a deep understanding of the psychological motivations of individuals and groups and an instinctive ability to deal with and manipulate them. People with this position have an instinct for the right thing to say or do, and when to do it, and, possibly even more important, what not to say and not to do.

This position is a testimony to a long life and a long career, giving an ability to roll with the punches, a deep inner resiliency that sustains them through dry periods and enables them to rise again for a fresh effort when the time is right. It may or may not contribute to a thirst for power, but it definitely gives an understanding of the functions and uses of power, and though they may not seek it for themselves, they are quite adept at manipulating those who have it in order to get what they need or want. If there are oppositions or squares to Pluto from the Sun or Mars, they may take a pugnacious attitude towards authority, challenging it or vilifying it, especially in youth, but in general, they are more inclined to make use of it than to fight it.

In most cases, this position guarantees a certain measure of ease and comfort, an ability to have or keep whatever is wanted by knowing who to speak to in private and what strings to pull. Actually, it is more preventive of loss than contributive to gain.

It is excellent for politicians, giving them the ability to make the right connections, and to manipulate others behind the scenes in "smoke-filled rooms" and by private phone calls, and by the instinctive understanding of what their constituency wants to hear (although the necessary public manner must come from other sectors). It enables all who have it to deal with politics at work and in the other areas of life where it can be troublesome.

Pluto in the Ninth House

For those with Pluto in the ninth, politics is their Achilles' heel. Either they are afraid of it and shy away from any dealings that smack of political maneuvering, or they go into it with the idea of changing things and get hurt in the process. They generally exhibit a cynical attitude toward politics or any kind of political dealings, yet they themselves are among the most instinctively adept when it comes to manipulating others to get what they want or to get out of what they don't want. Even so, they have a tendency to get caught in political dilemmas and lose thereby. They have a broad streak of righteousness that can surface under stress, causing them to say and do things that can make enemies, often silent ones, that work against them behind the scenes. They have a genuine desire to do good and accomplish good works, but must be careful how they go about it and not offend broad-based interest groups of long standing until their own structure is sound and can withstand a siege. They have a tendency to fly in the face of authority over some immediate issue, which brings about nothing but their own loss of face.

They have a great thirst for freedom and bitterly resent any encroachment upon it, real or imagined. They are generally fearful of getting involved in any group endeavors involving the signing of papers, lawyers, etc., fearing that someone may be pulling a fast one on them. This paranoia can put them at a disadvantage; it can make them hold back from worthwhile opportunities and cause them to put their trust in those who are clever at manipulating their fears to their own advantage.

Part of their nature craves the limelight and feels a great urge to step forth and proclaim the truth as they see it, and part of it is terrified of exposure and all the dangerous or embarrassing situations it might bring about. The tension of this ambiguity can cause them to behave very oddly when and if they do step forward. It also makes it hard for them to fight for an issue because they will surge forward at one moment, then hold back at the next.

Pluto in the Tenth House

Extremely single-minded in doing what they want to do, those with Pluto in the tenth will let nothing stand in their way once they have decided what they want to do and be. Sometimes this shows as a firm determination *not* to do what others want them to, particularly in youth, before they know what it is they want. It is hard for them to know what they want in youth because it is often something very unique that rises out of the socio-economic-psychological nature of the times. No failures, however crushing; no sidetracks, however tortuous and time-consuming; no handicaps, however crippling, can deter them from their ultimate goal once they have determined what it is. Their will grips onto the image of themselves in a certain role and nothing, not even their own good sense, can change it. Their imagination builds castles in the air that they must drive themselves to make real.

They are far-seeing, both back into the past and ahead to the future, and this can set them apart from their fellows and make them appear peculiar to others with more ordinary or immediate goals. There is apt to be quite a bit of loneliness along the way until they find others who understand, and even when they do, the demands of their fate often require that they part company.

This often testifies to a difficult start in life; the early loss of one or both parents, or similar external circumstances that shatter the peace and calm of the family and set them on their own, psychologically if not physically, at an early age. They are rarely seekers of power for its own sake, tending to be shy and constrained in front of groups, but they may seek it as a means to their own personal ends. They are capable of disregarding any and all ordinary demands placed on them by society, but are also capable of working nonstop around the clock for years toward their own personal goals, putting up with situations that would deter most others, if they feel that it will ultimately lead to their destiny.

It is a partial testament to a long, healthy life, particularly when their goal is one that cannot be reached in one lifetime, as though they can't take time out for sickness or death. If fate or fortune allows them to achieve their goal fairly early, they may die young. If there are oppositions to Pluto from the fourth, from the Sun, Mars, or Pluto's dispositor, they may die before their goal has been reached, or before they have found out what it is, but this is usually more due to the psychological stress of being so unique and lonely than to frustration over barriers in their path.

They have magnificent imaginations, almost a sixth sense about the nature of reality, that enables them to grasp the possibilities inherent in whatever it is that interests them.

They have passionate love natures. Their lives may be filled with unique love affairs which may be long and drawn out. They may have to overcome barriers to possess their beloved, and this may go on into old age, or happen more than once.

Pluto in the Eleventh House

This is an excellent position for Pluto. People with this placement are in a position to help further the goals of their entire generation. Those who must work alone may have their work used as a foundation for those who come later. It is not hard for them to set their egos aside and dedicate their efforts to the general good as long as they can be sure that their associates are doing likewise, but they will not participate for long in any group effort that isn't dedicated to some great goal.

They are apt to be lone wolves, content to go their own way, serene in the approval of one of two whom they respect. Even when they work with a group towards a goal, they often prefer to do their part alone and in their own way. They are pragmatic and realistic, interested in reality and how it works. This applies to all levels, from the scientific or material level of how something works physically; to the emotional levels, how people feel and why; to the spiritual, the purpose of life. They are Karma yogis; students of life who learn by observing the results of their actions.

They are usually handier with tools than with words. They are not generally good at small talk, though they may be very funny or witty. To them, talk is to be used mostly to transfer information. They tend to get silent or bored by trivial conversation and begin to yearn for something to do. School is usually boring to them unless they can take a lot of dance, drama, art, music, shop, anything where they can learn by doing. Rather than build castles in the air, their imagination helps them unravel the secrets of reality, the fruits of which are works: useful objects, inventions, superior methods and systems. They are usually handy and pick up physical skills quickly. They like to have as much control over their environment as they can, doing their own maintenance, making their own utensils, tools, etc., and puzzling things out for themselves, or trying to, before seeking assistance.

Pluto in the Twelfth House

This is a good place for Pluto, out of the way where it won't attract trouble, and above the horizon so it won't build up too much internal pressure. It brings the same single-minded devotion to the inner voice as it brings in the first house, but not the obstructions or the difficulties with making contact with the outer world. There is the same inability to follow the herd, but they are usually able to find an opening so that they can continue to pursue their own path, even from the beginning, frequently due to the assistance of a sympathetic parent or family.

This position gives the ability to maintain a strict regimen of daily work or training without assistance, if necessary, though usually an appropriate coach, teacher, or mentor is found who can give instructions, guidance, or even just occasional advice. They generally don't enjoy taking instruction, preferring to figure things out for themselves, though they are capable of taking orders if convinced that it's necessary. There is a soldierlike ability to maintain a rigorous or even painful schedule for long periods of time in order to accomplish some goal. Sometimes a means of livelihood will be chosen partly because it demands an ascetic lifestyle.

These qualities make this an excellent position for performers of all kinds, as well as ministers, and social leaders. They contribute to a subliminal understanding of what approach and subject matter will be of most compelling interest to their generation. This position also gives an innate understanding of body language and nonverbal communication, so that they can say more with a look, or a pause, then most can say with a paragraph. The inability to follow the herd or go any way but their own makes this a poor position for a politician.

It is a good position for anyone in the medical or helping professions as it gives an instinct for doing what will work to help or heal those in need; something that can't be taught in any school.

Rectification

Although the process is time-consuming, this book can assist in the rectification of a chart when the personality and life history of the individual is well known to the astrologer.

First, do a solar chart of the individual so that you have in front of you the basic sign locations and the major aspects linking the planets.

Next, on a sheet of rectangular paper turned so that it is wider than it is long, make a list down the left side of the paper of the planets in the order that they occur in this book, spacing them so that they fill the page from top to bottom with relatively equal space between each word. Across the top of the paper, write the numbers "1" through "12." These numbers refer to the houses. When you are finished, you will have a space on the paper for each possible position of a planet in a house. You may have to draw it up a couple of times until you get all the names and house numbers evenly spaced.

Read through the book and, after you have read each house position, note on your paper how well that particular house position fits the person whose chart you are rectifying. For example, you might use a scale of 1 to 5, where 1 means that the description of that position fits the person extremely well and 5 that it doesn't fit at all. Or perhaps the use of terms such as "excellent, good, okay, so-so, and no way," with an occasional "terrific!" will work better for you.

Do not make an effort to score at least one "1" or "excellent" for each planet or to resist putting down two "excellents" if both seem pertinent. Simply mark each position as you feel it while you're reading about it, keeping the nature and personality of the person whose chart it is in mind as you read.

When you have finished the book, go through the lists and make a separate list of all the highest scores. Next, compare this list with the solar chart. Turn the chart this way and that. Chances are that there is one rising sign that will include most or many of the house positions that you have marked with a "1" or "2" or an "excellent" or "good." In some cases, a small adjustment forward or backward will put a planet over the cusp into the house where it scores a "1" or an "excellent."

Once you have the rising sign that includes more of the meaningful house positions than any other, read again all the house positions from Moon to Pluto as they fall in this tentative chart. If there is a choice between two or more rising signs, reading through both of them should help you to decide. It is a time-consuming process, but for those charts we have yearned to have for years, it is worth it.

This process can also be useful in testing the validity of charts rectified by other methods.

Basic Principles for Beginners

Alone among the sciences, astrology is studied purely and simply because it works. Often called the mother of all science, it was the ancient matrix out of which all the hard sciences and basic math processes arose. It has only been within the past two hundred years or so that there has been any distinction between astronomy and astrology. Whenever you read "astronomer" in a book about things that happened over two hundred years ago, you can be sure that the individual in question was as much an astrologer as an astronomer.

Although astrology is the oldest science of all, no teaching exists that can state with any confidence why or how it works. In this, it is oddly similar to the science of electronics. Perhaps someday, through an increased understanding of the nature and effects of electromagnetic fields brought by working with electronics, a merging of the insights of both electronics and astrology will lead us to that Holy Grail of all hard science—the Unified Field Theory.

Although astrology is extremely complex and has many branches and a great variety of techniques (some at variance with each other), at its most basic it is the study of the planets in their relationship to each other and to the Earth, and the effect that they have on the Earth and on all living things that occupy its surface.

Like Russian nesting dolls, there are three levels of astrology that must be taken into consideration when doing horoscopes. The outermost shell is the zodiac, the background of constellations and stars against which the planets move. Next is the level of the planets themselves, among which we include the Sun, which is of course not a planet at all in the sense that astronomers use the term, but a star (albeit a small one); and the Moon, which is the Earth's satellite. In astrology, "planet" is a general term for all heavenly bodies that generate effects. In recent years, several of the asteroids have begun to be taken seriously by astrologers. These are not planets either, but what are thought to be chunks of an exploded or unformed planet. The third and innermost level of astrology is that of the Earth itself.

We divide the outermost level, the zodiac, into "signs" such as Aries, Taurus, and so on. There are twelve signs, consisting of thirty degrees each, that form a complete circle of 360 degrees which encompasses the entire solar system. Against this backdrop of signs, the planets move along their orbits, all more or less in the same plane, known as *the plane of the ecliptic*. As they move, they create and dissolve dynamic geometric relationships with each other and with the Earth, relationships we call "aspects" in astrology. It is through these aspects that we experience the effects of astrology on our lives.

At the center, on the innermost level, the Earth itself is divided into twelve "houses," each house approximating one two-hour segment of the day. Because of the dynamics of the Earth's motion, these houses are numbered backward; the first house represents the two-hour period before dawn, the second house the wee small hours of the night, the third house the two hours after midnight, the fourth house the two-hour period leading up to midnight, and so forth.

Numerous house systems have been devised over the centuries, many of which are still in use. Currently, the Koch system is rapidly replacing the Placidus system in popularity among astrologers, but there are others still in use.

The Horoscope

A horoscope, or chart, is a schematic drawing (similar to a map) of the relationship of the planets to the Earth and to each other at the moment of our birth, or at any other significant moment that we may wish to study. Our birth chart is the cornerstone of any astrological study we may do, because it is primarily to understand ourselves and each other that we study astrology today.

To create or "erect" a chart requires precise mathematical calculations. For hundreds of years, these were laboriously calculated by the astrologer from tables of logarithms, but now are usually performed almost instantaneously and far more accurately by computers. The time, in hours and minutes, and the place, in latitude and longitude, of the event in question (such as one's birth) gives the sign and the degree of that sign for each of the cusps of the twelve houses, as well as the sign and degree for each of the planets. Further positions are calculated for certain "points," such as the Moon's nodes. These are not planets, but are felt to be "sensitive spots" due to some action of the matrix in which all this energy functions. Many astrologers now include the five largest asteroids as well: Chiron, Juno, Pallas, Ceres, and Vesta.

The chart is complete, but now it must be interpreted. To do this, the astrologer relies on an understanding of the nature of the planets, the meanings of the houses, the effects of interplanetary aspects, and a host of other factors that allow a coherent picture to emerge from a complex set of interacting energies.

The Nature of the Planets

The Moon appears to move much more quickly than any of the other planets because, as the Earth's own satellite, it is so much closer than the others. Circling the Earth in about twenty-eight days, it spends roughly two-and-a-half days in each sign. Due to its speed, it creates more aspects than any other planet.

Mercury is the closest planet to the Sun, from our perspective always within thirty degrees ahead of or behind the Sun; which means that it appears to circle the zodiac in about the same amount of time as the Sun; a little over or a little less than a year. It can spend anywhere from two weeks to one-and-a-half months in a sign.

Venus occupies the orbit between Mercury and the Earth. Like Mercury, from our perspective on Earth it seems to accompany the Sun through the zodiac, never more than sixty degrees ahead of or behind the Sun. When it is ahead of the Sun, we call it the Morning Star because it rises ahead of the Sun at dawn. When it is behind the Sun, we call it the Evening Star because it hovers over the horizon after the Sun has set. It takes anywhere from slightly over three weeks to approximately three months to traverse a sign.

The Earth is next, and is the frame of reference from which we observe and measure the apparent motion of all the other planets.

The Sun appears to us to be next in line of the planets, and our measure of a year is the amount of time it takes for the Sun to move through the zodiac and return to a given starting point. In our culture, the New Year takes place in the sign Capricorn, but other cultures have defined the New Year as occurring at other points on the celestial calendar.

Mars is the first planet that lies outside the Earth/Sun circle, the first one that passes by the Earth from the side that faces out into Space. From our perspective on Earth, Mars circles the zodiac in two years and two months. The amount of time it spends in each sign varies between about five weeks to over seven months. Mars is the last of the inner, or *inferior*, planets (inferior refers to location, not to importance). Between Mars and Jupiter lies the asteroid belt, which is filled with bits and pieces of an exploded or unformed planet.

Jupiter is the first of the outer, or *superior*, planets; it is huge in comparison to any of the inner planets, with a mass three hundred times the mass of Earth and a volume a thousand times greater. Jupiter is thought by the Theosophists to be a proto-sun. It has at least fourteen satellites, is made up chiefly of hot gas, and even sheds a little inner light of its own. From our viewpoint, it takes Jupiter roughly twelve years to orbit the zodiac, spending about a year in each sign.

Saturn is next, somewhat smaller than Jupiter, but the most visually dramatic, thanks to its huge equatorial disk of gas and dust. From our perspective, Saturn takes close to twenty-eight years to orbit the zodiac and spends roughly two-and-a-half years in each sign. Saturn is the last of the seven ancient planets, the farthest that can be seen from Earth by the naked eye.

Uranus is next after Saturn. It is just about four times the size of the Earth. It was the first of the modern planets (those that had to wait for the perfection of the modern telescope) to be discovered. Uranus is perhaps the most dramatically different of the planets, in that its polar axis is not perpendicular to the ecliptic, as are those of the other planets, but lies within it (the plane of the ecliptic is the plane in which most planets and asteroids orbit the Sun). Uranus takes eighty-four years to orbit the Sun, spending roughly seven years in each sign of the zodiac.

Neptune is similar to Uranus in size, but its orbit lies beyond it. Neptune takes one-and-two-thirds centuries to orbit the zodiac, spending roughly fourteen years in each sign sign of the zodiac.

Pluto is the farthest planet of the zodiac, and the last to be discovered (so far). Its discovery had to wait for the development of photography (1931). Pluto's unique quality is the extreme eccentricity of its orbit, which is the most tilted from the plane of the ecliptic of all the planets. It also has the most extremely elongated orbit, so that Pluto gets much further proportionately from the Sun at aphelion (point of furthest remove from the Sun on any orbit) compared to perihelion (closest point) than any of the other planets. Pluto takes well over two centuries to orbit the Earth, spending from twelve to twenty-five years in each sign zodiac.

Which planets have the most influence on us? That depends. The inner planets have influence because of their proximity, the outer planets because of their size and the greater length of time it takes for aspects to form and dissolve. Planets are stronger in signs where they can function to the fullest of their capacity than they are in signs that don't give them what they need. They are strengthened by location near angles, particularly the first and tenth house cusps. They are strengthened by having the Sun or the Ascendant in those signs in which they are strongest. All planets are strengthened by aspects with other planets, even if strengthened to function in a difficult way. The weakest planet is one that is in a sign that doesn't work well with it, is below the horizon, far from an angle, and forms no aspects to any other planet.

The Nature of the Houses

A horoscope chart shows a circle that represents the zodiac, or background of cosmic influences, divided like a pie into twelve segments. These twelve divisions represent the *houses,* twelve two-hour segments of the day and, at the same time, a division of our lives into twelve categories.

It is this division into houses that is the most mystical of all astrological methods and has caused the most disagreement on the subject of what is fundamental. The twelve pie segments meet at a central point, a point which, in a natal chart, represents both the spot on the Earth where the individual was born and the moment in time when they were born. It also represents the individual himself or herself. If it is the chart for an event, the central point represents the time and the place where the event occurred (or will occur) and, for purposes of chart interpretation, the event itself.

The horizontal line that connects the first house with the seventh house cusp ("cusp" is a term used in astrology to mean edge, or demarcation of a house) represents the horizon, or the surface of the Earth, with the first house cusp as the easternmost point and the seventh house cusp as the westernmost point. Planets near the first house cusp are said to be "rising" because they are coming up over the eastern horizon at the time for which the chart was drawn. This is the most powerful location for a planet. Planets near the seventh house cusp are said to be "setting" because they are just going down into the lower half of the chart. The area below the horizon is the night half of the chart; the area above is the day half.

The topmost point of the chart, somewhere near the tenth house cusp, represents noon. Planets located near this point, known as the *Midheaven,* are said to be "culminating." This is the second-most powerful location for a planet. The lowest point on the chart, somewhere near the cusp of the fourth house, represents midnight. These four points—the cusps of the first, fourth, seventh, and tenth houses—are known as "the angles," and planets located on them have a great deal of power, particularly when near the first and tenth house cusps.

The twelve houses of the horoscope reflect, in many ways, the same principles shown by the twelve signs of the zodiac.

The first house is generally considered to affect the appearance and the personality as it is perceived by the outside world, as well as one's basic health. It shares with the Sun location the essentials of a person's basic nature. With important planets in the first house, a person will be self-involved and, unless severely blocked psychologically, quite determined to get their own way.

The second house is thought to affect one's resources and sense of values, a sense of place, and the quality and amount of self-esteem. It indicates the personal environment and surroundings. A well-populated second house generally shows someone acquisitive in nature (though this is strongly modified by the nature of the planets and the aspects to them). It is also clear from this study that it has a great deal to do with an individual's sexual nature. It is a hidden, or silent, sector, operating chiefly behind the scenes.

The third house has to do with siblings, neighbors, young people, school (particularly early school experiences), and relationships with people who live nearby or whom one sees on a daily basis through work or other routine. It also has to do with cars, cabs, subways, bicycles, and short trips, as well as team sports, especially those taught at school. It has to do with basic learning and affects the ability to communicate. People with lots of planets in the third house like to be around other people. For these individuals, self-imposed solitude is not healthy or natural behavior.

The fourth house rules the home, family, and roots. It concerns one's ancestors, heritage, and parents. In our Western culture it usually indicates the father, the parent from whom we take our name and our sense of importance or legitimacy. It also has to do with land, real estate, gardens and farms, and one's house or apartment. Interior decorating, furniture, and so forth is the province of the fourth house. This is where one puts down roots, takes hold, fights off intruders, digests one's dinner and the day's experience, and relaxes in the peace of intimacy. Traditionally, it also has information about the ends of things; the end of life in a natal chart, or the final result in an event chart.

The fifth house rules romantic relationships, sexual intercourse, conception, childbirth, one's own children and students. It also represents hobbies, private workshops, creative efforts, art and performance studios, the theatre, dance, drama, music, and art. It is the house of self-fulfillment, of doing as one pleases. Lots of planets in the fifth house indicates a person with a charismatic personality who energizes others by their very presence.

The sixth house rules work and service, jobs, health, employers and employees, dependents, pets and other small animals (as well as insects, vermin, and pests in general, including your tiresome neighbor), the workplace, offices, office buildings, secretaries, and other office workers. It is the house of duty, dedication, and maintenance. It is the door of knowledge gained through repetitive, mundane examination of data, and wisdom and compassion gained through service to others, whether rendered gladly or forced by karma. With a lot of planets in the sixth, work, health and dependability are issues.

The seventh house rules the partner or mate, partnerships in general, marriage, divorce, and open enemies. It is the house of one's opposite, of "the other" that both repels and attracts, entices and frightens. It is the door of knowledge gained by experiencing events not of one's own making. It is the chief entry point of karma. It has to do with board rooms, council chambers, courtrooms, lawyers, and judges. Lots of planets in the seventh house means lots of relationships, lots of trips to court, lots of ups, lots of down, lots of everything.

The eighth house rules secrets, death, near-death experiences, taxes, banks, loans, the partner's money, the partner's sexuality, and events that come through the partner's sex life. It rules inheritance, foundation grants, the occult, and ESP or out-of-the-body experiences. It is a hidden, or silent, sector, operating behind the scenes, regarding matters that no one but the native knows about. It has much to do with Fate, and may indicate important past-life events. Many planets in the eighth indicates someone whom no one can really know.

The ninth house has to do with long-distance travel and higher education, particularly in science and philosophy, but in all the liberal arts as well. It has to do with religion, politics, and the need to go beyond the confines of the routine of home/family/job. It rules hiking boots and backpacks as well as telescopes and microscopes. It relates to politicians, the clergy, professors, yogis, saints, foreigners, and travelers. It refers to churches, temples, universities, colleges, think tanks, study groups, and the buildings that house them. It also rules airplanes, trains, ocean liners, communication satellites, telephones, air-mail, e-mail, macro and micro-photography, and all external and internal means of reaching beyond the ordinary confines of existence to bring home fascinating and unusual truths about faraway places and that clockwork orange we call the universe.

The tenth house is traditionally called the house of career. In a natal chart, it shows one's reputation with people whom one does not know personally. It testifies to the arc of influence created by the life effort, if it be high or low, for personal or general good or ill. In a natal chart, it also speaks to the native's relationship with their parents, especially the parent (in our culture typically the mother) who instills a desire to reach beyond what has been inherited. Many planets inhabiting the tenth house usually guarantees a strong career effort.

The eleventh house is considered the house of friendship and dreams. It concerns long-term friendships based on mutual interest rather than just proximity, and the dreams we translate into goals or plans when we can. It speaks to our relationship with our surrounding community, for only through community and the help of those who share our visions can we make our dreams come true. Many planets in the eleventh house guarantee many social contacts and often the ability to bring off large-scale schemes.

The twelfth house has been called, with the dour accuracy of astrological tradition, "the house of self-undoing." Certainly it is that, but also more than that. Here we find clues to the areas of life that require patient self-study or perhaps therapy. Like the eighth house, this is a hidden sector of the chart. None but partners, family, and the closest friends will be likely to know what happens here. On the surface level, it rules large public institutions such as hospitals, sanatoria, prisons, and the most Dickensian of government bureaucracies. It also rules large (and therefore potentially dangerous) animals like horses, rhinos, elephants, sharks, and whales. People with lots of planets in the twelfth house have the opportunity to resolve a great deal of karma in this life.

Aspects

Aspects are the dynamic geometric relationships that are continually forming and dissolving between the Earth and the other planets. It takes at least two planets (plus the Earth) to make an aspect. Aspects have traditionally been divided into two categories: bad and good, hard and easy, or difficult and harmonious. There is no workable way around this distinction, but it must be kept in mind that "crisis" and opportunity are two sides of the same coin and that omelets can't be made without breaking eggs. An ideal chart, if there is such a thing, is a combination of hard and easy aspects; the hard for energy and drive, the easy for the balance and timing that comes from a relaxed, accepting attitude. The question is always: How are the various aspects, hard and easy, blended; how do they work together?

If there are too many hard aspects, the native may have to struggle so hard to find a way out that they may either give up or become too hardened, too forceful; while with nothing but easy aspects they may never be challenged enough to grow. Also, what is good and what is bad? What is a successful life and what is a failure? This is where astrology leaves the realm of science and enters that of art and philosophy; where astrological interpretation rubs up against the many theories of personality, both religious and scientific, that have been put forth over the centuries. It has been said that the charts of the most evolved people will include all the planets in aspect to each other, with none left out. I haven't had a chance to check this out thoroughly, but it sounds like an interesting idea.

The major aspects used by most astrologers consist of the following:

The opposition, an angle of of 180 degrees, is generally considered to be the most difficult aspect. It occurs when the Earth stands between two planets, which pull on it from opposing directions, like the children's game of monkey-in-the-middle. This aspect is like yin-yang, a push-pull that is difficult but dynamic, as the planets seem to vie with each other for ascendancy. It brings events into the life that demand resolution.

The square is the most dynamic aspect. It can be equally as difficult as the opposition, depending on the planets involved. (Sometimes it can even seem more so.) A square is formed when the Earth is the apex of a ninety degree angle between two other planets. This is a frictional aspect rather than a sundering aspect like the opposition. Things don't fall apart here, but it seems as though they might. One feels like one is caught in traffic, forced to go places and do things that one doesn't always prefer, sometimes moving too fast for comfort, sometimes getting stuck, unable to move at all. Situations seem to jab at us continually until we change our position in some way. Many squares in a chart means a life of constant change and evolution. Without a lot of work at developing patience and forbearance, this can indicate a difficult personality.

The inconjunct is in many ways the most tiresome aspect. (In older astrology books, it is sometimes referred to as the *quincunx,* a tiresome word.) Here, the Earth is at the apex of a 150 degree angle. This is an aspect of hidden tension. Not as powerful as the opposition or square, it lingers in the background of the chart, causing irritating difficulties. It is an aspect of sacrifice, where matters ruled by the weaker of the planets are continually forced to give way to the matters of the stronger. With the opposition, events would force an open confrontation, decision, and adjustment, but with the inconjunct, nothing ever comes to a head. Never totally disabling, it often leads to some form of therapy, to a search for psychologically coming to terms with the external world, or to an interest in religion or philosophy as an answer to life's troubles.

The trine is generally considered to be the most harmonious aspect. In this, the Earth is at the apex of a 120 degree angle with two other planets. This is an aspect of easy flow. It carries a sensation of effortless rising, like a bird coasting in the airstream wake of a ship, or a sailboat traveling with the wind. The ideal aspect for accomplishment is an opposition or square with a trine connected to one of the planets.

The sextile of sixty degrees is also considered to be harmonious, though somewhat less so than the trine. It is an aspect of support, not freedom like the trine. The sextile promises support but also requires support in exchange. There is an aspect of take as well as give to the sextile.

The conjunction is an angle of zero degrees, where one planet stands in front of or behind another as seen from the Earth. This aspect can be hard or easy, depending on the planets involved and the sign and house they are in. Usually it is a mixed bag, with some good and some difficult effects. A conjunction of Venus with Pluto or Saturn is mostly difficult. A conjunction of Saturn and Mars can be very good in some ways. When there are more than two planets close together in this way, it is known as a *stellium* and becomes a primary feature of the chart, particularly if the Sun, Moon, the Sun's dispositor, or the ruler of the ascendant is involved.

Retrogradation

Retrogradation is the *apparent backward motion* of a planet that occurs when the Earth appears to pull ahead of it, and pass it, a phenomenon similar to the way an inside runner on a track may appear to be ahead of a runner on an outside track, although this is only an appearance, due to the fact that the track of the inside runner is *shorter* than the outer tracks. From the perspective of the inside runner, the outside runner may appear to be slowing down. It is these periods of apparent slowing that give the appearance, from the perspective of Earth, that the retrograde planet is actually moving backward. These periods of retrogradation cause the widely differing times that a planet may spend in a sign. Retrogradation affects the nature of a planet in a horoscope by causing the energies involved to be more internalized than they typically would be.

Delineation

These descriptions barely scratch the surface of the chief concepts in astrology, but they should be enough so that, if you have a chart drawn up by a professional astrologer, with the names and house positions of the planets written out for you, you will be able to grasp most of what is put forth in the following paragraphs. For more detail, I recommend that you ask at your local bookstore about a good beginning astrology book.

The first step in delineating a chart is to determine which are the strongest planets. Then you should figure out which planets have aspects, and what these aspects are.

As for the strength of the planets, apart from locations near angles, planets are strong if they are strong in, or *rule,* the sign the Sun is located in. Jupiter is very strong in Sagittarius, so Jupiter has always been known as the "ruler" of Sagittarius. Modern astrology soft-pedals the notion of rulership, and rightly so, because it has caused a number of dubious ideas to become accepted as fact. Still, every planet is at its best in one sign, its worst in another sign (usually the sign *opposite* that in which it is best), and good or not so good in other signs. A planet is also given extra strength if it's strongest sign is rising. In that case, it is known as the *ruler of the ascendant.*

Once the nature of the planets and of the signs has been thoroughly absorbed, it is easy to see, for instance, how the Moon would naturally be powerful in Cancer and conversely be forced to struggle for expression in the opposite sign, Capricorn. If the Sun in a birth chart is located in Sagittarius, then Jupiter, as the *ruler* of Sagittarius, is considered to be the Sun's *dispositor.* Therefore, Jupiter is an important planet in this chart, no matter where it is located. If it is located below the horizon in the chart, in a poor sign for Jupiter, such as Capricorn, and without aspects to any other planet (which is very unusual), then the astrologer knows that this person will have a tough row to hoe in life. A weakly positioned and aspected Sun can be greatly strengthened by a well-placed and aspected dispositor. In contrast, discipline and will power will be needed to make up for a weak dispositor of the Sun, even if the Sun itself is strong.

For a chart to be "good," there should be a balance among the elements, meaning that there should be at least one or two planets each in the fire, earth, air, and water signs, and the same in each of the cardinal, fixed, and mutable signs. A "perfect" chart would also have some planets above the horizon and some below, some in the eastern half and some in the west; all of which, needless to say, rarely happens.

It must be kept in mind that a horoscope, or chart, is like the photo taken at a horse race to determine the winner. It is an image of a dynamic event or series of events that continue after the moment defined by the chart. Therefore, if a planet is within five degrees of the next house cusp, you should read the paragraphs for that house position as well. However, if a planet is within five degrees of the preceding house, don't read that position unless the planet is retrograde, because planets cast their energy ahead but not behind. As natal planets move forward by progression, they will come to reside in the following house, but only retrograde planets (and the Moon's nodes) will move toward the preceding house.

LOOK FOR THE CRESCENT

Llewellyn publishes hundreds of books on your favorite subjects! To get these exciting books, check your local bookstore or order them directly from Llewellyn.

ORDER BY PHONE
- Call toll-free within the U.S. and Canada, 1-800-THE MOON
- In Minnesota, call (651) 291-1970
- We accept VISA, MasterCard, and American Express

ORDER BY MAIL
- Send the full price of your order (MN residents add 7% sales tax) in U.S. funds, plus postage & handling to:

  Llewellyn Worldwide
  P.O. Box 64383, Dept. K108–2
  St. Paul, MN 55164–0383, U.S.A.

POSTAGE & HANDLING
(For the U.S., Canada, and Mexico)
- $4 for orders $15 and under
- $5 for orders over $15
- No charge for orders over $100

We ship UPS in the continental United States. We ship standard mail to P.O. boxes. Orders shipped to Alaska, Hawaii, the Virgin Islands, and Puerto Rico are sent first-class mail. Orders shipped to Canada and Mexico are sent surface mail.

International orders: Airmail—add freight equal to price of each book to the total price of order, plus $5.00 for each non-book item (audio tapes, etc.).

Surface mail—Add $1.00 per item.

Allow 4–6 weeks for delivery on all orders.
Postage and handling rates subject to change.

DISCOUNTS
We offer a 20% discount to group leaders or agents who order a minimum of 5 copies of the same book.

FREE CATALOG
Get a free copy of our color catalog, *New Worlds of Mind and Spirit*. Subscribe for just $10.00 in the United States and Canada ($30.00 overseas, airmail). Many bookstores carry *New Worlds*—ask for it!

Visit our website at www.llewellyn.com for more information.